STUDENT STUDY GUIDE

to Accompany

Comer *Abnormal Psychology*

STUDENT STUDY GUIDE

to Accompany
Comer *Abnormal Psychology*

Norris D. Vestre
Arizona State University

W. H. FREEMAN AND COMPANY
NEW YORK

ISBN 0-7167-2298-4

Printed in the United States of America

1 2 3 4 5 6 7 8 9 0 KP 9 9 8 7 6 5 4 3 2

CONTENTS

TO THE STUDENT

This *Student Study Guide* is designed as a supplement to *Abnormal Psychology* by Ronald J. Comer. Its purpose is to assist you in learning the material covered in the textbook. More specifically, its intent is to help you to study more efficiently, master the textbook's contents, and thereby prepare for course examinations.

The *Student Study Guide* is organized to parallel the chapters of the textbook. Each chapter of the guide contains a chapter overview, a list of key terms, sample multiple-choice questions, sample short-answer questions, a section providing further explanation of difficult material, and a list of suggested readings.

When read before the corresponding chapter in the text, the chapter overview provides an orientation to the corresponding material in the book. When read later, the chapter overview acts as a summary and reexamination of chapter content. The list of key terms provides a different form of orientation and review. Most of the terms listed appear in boldface print in the textbook and need to be understood to master the subject matter of the book. Many of the terms are also to be found in the glossary of the textbook. It is important that each term be studied within the context of the chapter in which it appears.

The sample test questions include 10 multiple-choice and 20 short-answer questions, with the correct answers printed at the end of each chapter. You should test yourself on these questions, that is, try to answer them from memory, *after* you have studied the material in the textbook chapter. The results of this "self-test" should then be used as a basis for deciding whether you need to work further on the chapter. The importance of attempting to assess your own knowledge and understanding cannot be overemphasized, and the appropriate use of the sample test questions is one way of doing this. A second way is to thumb through a chapter again, *after* having studied it, and use the boldface printed words and section headings as stimuli for asking yourself questions. You can, then, immediately check the text itself to determine if you have answered correctly. Reading the textbook, although obviously crucial, does tend to be a passive process. "Testing yourself" is a more active, and hence a more memorable, learning experience, as well as a good way to practice the kinds of skills that are required in taking course exams.

The material discussed in "Explanations of Difficult Material" is not always difficult, although many of these sections are indeed devoted to further explanations of subtle or complex concepts or ideas. In some of these sections, a concept or idea from the textbook was chosen for further exploration not so much for its difficulty as for its fundamental importance to the study of Abnormal Psychology.

The final section of each chapter of the *Student Study Guide* provides suggested additional readings. These selections, plus the textbook reference list, will be of use to those who wish to pursue a given topic in more detail whether for the purposes of completing a course assignment or out of personal interest in the subject.

CHAPTER 1

ABNORMAL PSYCHOLOGY: PAST AND PRESENT

CHAPTER OVERVIEW

The field of *abnormal psychology* is devoted to the study of abnormal behavior. Criteria for a diagnosis of abnormal mental functioning are *deviance, distress, dysfunction*, and *dangerousness* (to self or others). In general, behaviors, thoughts, or emotions that meet some combination of these criteria may be regarded as abnormal, although problems can be raised with each of the criteria.

Abnormal psychological functioning appears to have been present throughout recorded history, but the explanations for it have varied. In the ancient world abnormality was thought to be caused by evil spirits. Some Stone Age people practiced *trephination*, an operation in which a section of the skull was removed to allow evil spirits to escape. The Greeks and Romans attributed abnormal behavior to a variety of natural causes, and their physicians described such disorders as *melancholia* (persistent sadness), *mania* (frenzied excitement), *dementia* (decline in reasoning ability), *hysteria* (physical symptoms with no physical cause), *delusions* (blatantly false beliefs), and *hallucinations* (perceptions of imagined sights and sounds). After the fall of Rome, supernatural explanations came to the fore again. The demonological explanations of the Middle Ages were gradually replaced, again by medical views, but progress in the care of the mentally ill was slow, partly because of erroneous medical theory and partly because of fear and suspicion of the mentally ill.

In the late eighteenth century Philippe Pinel began to emphasize *moral treatment*, and a reform movement soon spread from France to England and the United States. Despite early apparent successes, however, a variety of factors—overcrowded hospitals, lack of funding, staff shortages, prejudice against the mentally ill, unrealistic expectations of cures—brought a decline in moral treatment. Support for the *somatogenic* (biological) *perspective* revived in the late nineteenth century. Research findings linking general paresis, an organic brain disorder, with syphilis, followed by Emil Kraepelin's efforts in the classification of mental disorders and his ideas regarding organic causation, contributed to this renewed interest in the somatogenic view of abnormality. Around the same time, the *psychogenic perspective* gained support as a result of the development of *hypnosis* to treat hysterical disorders, the demonstration that hysterical disorders could be induced by hypnosis, demonstrations by Josef Breuer and Sigmund Freud that psychological treatment could be effective in alleviating hysterical disorders, and especially the theoretical contributions of Freud. The patients of Freud and his followers received *outpatient therapy* in the therapist's office rather than hospital treatment.

The current era of abnormal psychology began in the 1950s, when *psychotropic medications* were introduced. Large numbers of patients were released from mental hospitals in the movement toward deinstitutionalization. Those who still required mental health services were to receive them at community centers. The *community mental health approach* can be seen as appropriate and reasonable, but its implementation has been a failure, at least so far as the seriously and chronically mentally ill are concerned. The efforts of mental health practitioners on behalf of patients whose problems are less severe have been more effective. Positive signs on the mental health front include the increased use of outpatient care, specialized programs focusing on one type of psychological problem, the emergence and advancement of additional theoretical perspectives, and an emphasis on systematic research. Today's mental health practitioners include *psychiatrists* (physicians who have completed a residency in the treatment of mental dysfunctions), *clinical psychologists, counseling psychologists, educational psychologists, psychiatric nurses,* and *psychiatric social workers.*

KEY TERMS

abnormal psychology

deviance

distress

dysfunction

dangerousness

trephination

melancholia

mania

dementia

hysteria

delusions

hallucinations

moral treatment

somatogenic perspective

psychogenic perspective

hypnosis

psychotropic medications

community mental health approach

psychiatrists

clinical psychologists

counseling psychologists

educational psychologists

psychiatric nurses

psychiatric social workers

SAMPLE
MULTIPLE-CHOICE
QUESTIONS

1. The fact that a society's values in regard to particular behaviors may change over time poses most problems for which criterion of abnormality?
   a. deviance
   b. distress
   c. dysfunction
   d. dangerousness

2. Which criterion of abnormality is based on the subject's self-report?
   a. deviance
   b. distress
   c. dysfunction
   d. dangerousness

3. The story about the group of people in Michigan who go swimming throughout the winter illustrates problems with which criterion of abnormality?
   a. deviance
   b. distress
   c. dysfunction
   d. dangerousness

4. Current statistics on abnormality in the United States indicate that approximately what percentage of individuals experience serious mental disorders?
   a. 40%
   b. 25%
   c. 10%
   d. 2%

5. Hippocrates believed that abnormal behavior was caused by:
   a. supernatural forces
   b. internal psychological factors
   c. internal medical problems
   d. all of the above

6. Pinel believed that the mentally ill should be treated:
   a. by prayer and meditation
   b. by isolation and rest
   c. by constructive manual labor
   d. with support and kindness

7. The method of treatment advanced by Pinel and Tuke is referred to as:
   a. sleep therapy
   b. community treatment
   c. crisis treatment
   d. moral treatment

8. Which of the following factors contributed to the decline of the moral treatment movement in the late nineteenth century?
   a. failure of some patients to benefit from moral treatment
   b. lack of funds to run hospitals properly
   c. prejudice against the mentally ill
   d. all of the above

9. Kraepelin, a German psychiatrist, is regarded as an important influence in the late nineteenth-century resurgence of the:
   a. psychogenic perspective
   b. somatogenic perspective
   c. behavioral perspective
   d. sociological perspective

10. Work with which mental disorder provided the impetus for the emergence of the psychogenic perspective?
    a. hysterical disorders
    b. general paresis
    c. schizophrenia
    d. melancholia

SAMPLE SHORT-ANSWER QUESTIONS

1. List the four criteria of abnormality.

   _____
   _____
   _____
   _____

2. Explicit and implicit rules for appropriate behavior that are established by a society are called

   _____.

3. Szasz proposed that the deviations that society calls mental illnesses are better referred to as

    _____.

4. Recent surveys of the United States population indicate that which two disorders are the most common?

    _____

    _____

5. Among the disorders that appeared during the Middle Ages were two in which large numbers of people shared the same delusions and hallucinations. These two disorders were called

    _____

    _____

6. Hippocrates proposed that abnormal behavior was caused by an imbalance of _____.

7. The person who is often called the father of American psychiatry is _____.

8. Philippe Pinel (about 1800) is credited with being the most influential figure in initiating _____ treatment.

9. The person who was instrumental in securing passage of laws mandating more humane care for the mentally ill in the United States was

    _____.

10. The person who was instrumental in bringing reforms and moral treatment for the mentally ill to England was

    _____.

11. The discovery of a causal link between syphilis and general paresis led researchers and practitioners to think that many or all mental illnesses might be due to _____ factors.

12. Kraepelin, a German psychiatrist and researcher, is credited with developing the first system of _____ abnormal behavior.

13. Mesmer's treatment technique, called *mesmerism*, was years later developed further and referred to as

    _____.

14. The demonstration that hysterical disorders could be induced in normal people during hypnosis was seen as evidence in support of the _____ perspective.

15. Freud's theoretical contributions to abnormal psychology can be seen as emphasizing the _____ perspective.

16. In the 1950s an important treatment for the severely mentally disturbed was the discovery of _____.

17. From the 1950s to the 1980s there was a shift in the percentage of people treated for psychological disorders as outpatients and as inpatients, so that inpatient treatment _____ and outpatient treatment _____.

18. Is the recent emergence of numerous, often competing theoretical perspectives a positive or negative development?

19. The physician who specializes in the diagnosis and treatment of the mentally ill is a(n)_____.

20. The psychologist who specializes in the assessment and treatment of the mentally ill is a(n)_____.

EXPLANATIONS OF DIFFICULT MATERIAL

Note that although there are four criteria to be considered when a person's normality or abnormality is to be assessed— deviance, distress, dysfunction, and dangerousness (the "four D's")—no one of these criteria applies to all cases of abnormality. One person who exhibits one of these characteristics may be judged to be abnormal; another who exhibits the same characteristic may be regarded as normal. Note also that the four criteria are not equally defensible. Dangerousness (to self and others) is rather infrequent among people who are judged to be psychologically abnormal by other criteria. Moreover, many people who are not regarded as psychologically abnormal are quite dangerous. Deviance probably applies to most people who are considered psychologically abnormal by the criterion of distress or dysfunction, but many people who are deviant are not abnormal by other criteria. Distress and dysfunction would seem to be the most defensible criteria, but even these can be shown to be problematic in a few instances.

It must be acknowledged that the concept of abnormality is only a rough practical notion, not a precise scientific construct. Definitional problems notwithstanding, at one time or another, families and neighbors as well as mental health professionals are required to decide whether someone is normal or abnormal. Some combination of the four D's guides these judgments.

ADDITIONAL READINGS

Kiesler, C. A., & Sibulkin, A. E. (1987). *Mental hospitalization: Myths and facts about a national crisis.* Newbury Park, Calif.: Sage.

Neugebauer, R. (1978). Treatment of the mentally ill in medieval and early modern England: A reappraisal. *Journal of the History of the Behavioral Sciences, 14,* 158–169.

Spanos, N. P. (1978). Witchcraft in histories of psychiatry: A critical appraisal and an alternative conceptualization. *Psychological Bulletin, 35,* 417–439.

Spanos, N. P., & Gottlieb, J. (1979). Demonic possession, mesmerism, and hysteria: A social psychological perspective on their historical interrelations. *Journal of Abnormal Psychology, 88,* 527–546.

Zilboorg, G., & Henry, G. (1941). *A history of medical psychology.* New York: Norton.

ANSWER KEY

Multiple-Choice Questions:

1a, 2b, 3a, 4b, 5c, 6d, 7d, 8d, 9b, 10a.

Short-Answer Questions:

1. deviance, distress, dysfunction, dangerousness
2. norms
3. problems of living
4. anxiety disorders, alcohol abuse (or substance abuse)

5.   tarantism, lycanthropy
6.   body humors
7.   Benjamin Rush
8.   moral
9.   Dorothea Dix
10. William Tuke
11. biological
12. classifying
13. hypnosis
14. psychogenic
15. psychogenic
16. psychotropic medications
17. decreased; increased
18. positive
19. psychiatrist
20. clinical psychologist

CHAPTER 2

MODELS OF PSYCHOLOGICAL ABNORMALITY

CHAPTER OVERVIEW

Paradigms, or *models,* are developed to explain abnormal behavior. Each model is an explicit set of concepts and propositions that indicates how abnormality is described and what causal factors are assumed.

The *biological model* assumes a link between anatomical structures and biochemical processes in the development of abnormal behavior. Some types of abnormality seem to have a genetic component. The effectiveness of psychotropic drugs may be interpreted as supportive of the biological model.

The *psychodynamic model* implicates unconscious psychological conflict as a critical factor in the development of abnormal behavior. The conflicts are considered to have originated in childhood experiences. The model's central concepts include the *id* (instinctual needs and impulses), the *superego* (conscience and ego ideal), and the *ego*. The ego serves as an arbitrator in conflicts between the opposing demands of the id and superego. Conflicts lead to anxiety, which leads to dysfunction and psychological abnormality. Freud proposed four developmental stages: the *oral stage,* when the infant's main gratification comes from the mouth; the *anal stage,* when the focus of pleasure shifts to the anus; the *phallic stage,* when boys develop an *Oedipus complex* and girls an *Electra complex*; the *latency stage* when sexual desires subside; and the *genital stage,* when sexual urges reemerge.

11

The *behavioral model* proposes that all human behavior, normal (adaptive) and abnormal (maladaptive), is learned. Moreover, the same principles of learning can explain the acquisition of all behavior patterns. Behaviorists focus on three types of learning: *classical conditioning, operant conditioning,* and *modeling.* One strength of the behavioral model is that behavioral explanations and treatments can be tested in the laboratory.

The *cognitive model* proposes that abnormality results from a variety of cognitive problems: maladaptive or irrational assumptions, specific upsetting thoughts, and illogical thinking processes. The therapy suggested by the cognitive model consists of efforts to modify maladaptive thoughts. The cognitive model also lends itself to laboratory testing, and research findings have supported the model.

The *humanistic-existential model* represents two distinct perspectives that share an emphasis on responsibility, self-determination, and accurate self-awareness. The *humanists* also believe that all persons have an innate tendency toward *self-actualization,* or development toward their potential. Lack of unconditional positive regard, conditions of worth, and distortions of experience lead to abnormal behavior. The *existentialists* believe that abnormality is caused by attempts to avoid life's responsibilities. The result of this path through life is an empty, inauthentic life characterized by negative emotions.

The *sociocultural model* of abnormal behavior focuses on the social and cultural environment of the individual. Sociocultural explanations have focused on family structure and communication, societal stress, and social labels and reactions. The model has made unique contributions to the understanding of abnormal behavior, among them *family systems theory,* which views the family as a system of interacting parts, and *family therapy,* which treats all members of the family, not just the one designated as "sick." The sociocultural model also focuses on societal stress and societal labels and reactions.

None of the models is capable of explaining the entire range of abnormal behavior. When one seeks to determine the cause of a disorder, it is useful to distinguish among *predisposing factors, precipitating factors,* and *maintaining factors.* Finally, clinicians are increasingly accepting a *diathesis-stress* explanation of abnormal behavior—the view that a biological, psychological, or sociocultural factor predisposes a person to a disorder, which is then precipitated by psychological stress and maintained by maladaptive thinking.

KEY TERMS

paradigms (models)

biological model

psychodynamic model

id

superego

ego

oral stage

anal stage

phallic stage

Oedipus complex

humanists

existentialists

sociocultural model

family systems theory

family therapy

Electra complex

latency stage

genital stage

behavioral model

classical conditioning

operant conditioning

modeling

cognitive model

humanistic-existential model

self-actualization

predisposing factors

precipitating factors

maintaining factors

diathesis-stress

SAMPLE
MULTIPLE-CHOICE
QUESTIONS

1. Which of the following terms has the same meaning as "paradigm"?
   a. measurement
   b. observation
   c. model
   d. none of the above

2. Kraepelin's views and his efforts at classification can be seen to contribute to the:
   a. biological model
   b. psychodynamic model
   c. sociocultural model
   d. cognitive model

3. The effectiveness of psychotropic drugs is seen as most clearly supporting which model of abnormality?
   a. biological
   b. psychodynamic
   c. behavioral
   d. cognitive

4. Which of the following disorders would be called functional mental disorders?
   a. mood disorders
   b. anxiety disorders
   c. both a and b
   d. neither a nor b

5. In his theory of psychoanalysis, Freud emphasized the central role of the:
    a. unconscious
    b. conscious
    c. preconscious
    d. actualizing tendency

6. In Freud's view, the second stage of development is the:
    a. oral stage
    b. anal stage
    c. latency stage
    d. trust stage

7. In Pavlov's classical conditioning experiment, salivation to the tone after conditioning trials represents a(n):
    a. US
    b. UR
    c. CS
    d. CR

8. One difference between the psychodynamic model and the behavioral model is that the behavioral model:
    a. regards behavior as determined by experience
    b. is more readily testable
    c. regards behavior as capable of being changed
    d. all of the above

9. Self-statements are central to which model of abnormality?
    a. psychodynamic
    b. behavioral
    c. cognitive
    d. humanistic-existential

10. Lack of unconditional positive regard early in life is expected to lead to:
    a. self-actualization
    b. conditions of worth
    c. both a and b
    d. neither a nor b

SAMPLE
SHORT-ANSWER
QUESTIONS

1. An explicit set of basic assumptions that helps explain other people's behavior is called a(n) _____.

2. Research that linked general paresis with syphilis provided support for the _____ model.

3. The brain is made up of nerve cells called _____.

4. Clinicians traditionally make a distinction between organic mental disorders and _____ mental disorders.

5. Neurotransmitter substances transmit a nerve impulse from one neuron to the next neuron across the _____.

6. The person credited with the formulation of the psychodynamic model is _____.

7. The psychodynamic model proposes that abnormal behavior is explained by _____.

8. The id operates in accordance with the _____ principle.

9. The two components of the superego are the _____ and the _____.

10. According to Freud, which stage of development establishes the foundation for adult functioning? _____

11. Which of Freud's developmental stages follows the anal stage? _____

12. In Pavlov's classical conditioning experiment, salivation to the food powder is called the _____.

13. In operant conditioning, the procedure of reinforcing successive approximations of the desired behavior is called _____.

14.	Albert Ellis and Aaron Beck contributed to the development of the _____ model.

15.	According to Carl Rogers, all humans have a basic need to receive _____ from significant others (especially their parents).

16.	Which model emphasizes psychological health rather than illness? _____

17.	Which model most strongly emphasizes that people are self-determining? _____

18.	Family systems theory and family therapy are consistent with the ideas of which model of abnormality?
_____

19.	Research has shown that the correlation between social change and the rate of abnormal functioning is
_____.

20.	Proponents of which model would argue that abnormal functioning is influenced by diagnostic labels?
_____

EXPLANATIONS OF DIFFICULT MATERIAL

The scientific method offers unparalleled advantages as a means of discovering truth about abnormal behavior, yet it is important to realize that the scientific enterprise is <u>not</u> completely objective. The paradigm or model chosen has crucial influence on any scientific activity. A model, once selected by a researcher, dictates the kinds of concepts and research methods that will be used. In fact, every decision concerning scientific inquiry is made within the constraints imposed by the model. Models of abnormality are, in effect, preconceptions about the domain of abnormality. The preconceptions embodied in the model of abnormality a particular scientist espouses place limits on what research methods are used, what observations are made, and how the findings are interpreted. It should be clear, then, that there is some subjectivity in science, as there is in other areas of life. Although the scientific method remains the most valid means to advance knowledge, it is important to be aware of the subjective elements in the process.

ADDITIONAL READINGS

Neugebauer, R. (1979). Medieval and early modern theories of mental illness. *Archives of General Psychiatry, 36,* 477–484.

Price, R. H. (1978). *Abnormal behavior: Perspectives in conflict* (2nd ed.). New York: Holt, Rinehart & Winston.

Rosenbaum, M., & Muroff, M. (Eds.) (1984). *Anna O.: Fourteen contemporary reinterpretations.* New York: Free Press.

Suppe, F. (1974). *The structure of scientific theories.* Urbana: University of Illinois Press.

ANSWER KEY

Multiple-Choice Questions:

1c, 2a, 3a, 4c, 5a, 6b, 7d, 8b, 9c, 10b.

Short-Answer Questions:

1. paradigm (or model or perspective)
2. biological
3. neurons
4. functional
5. synapse
6. Freud
7. unconscious processes (conflicts)
8. pleasure
9. conscience, ego ideal
10. genital stage
11. phallic stage
12. unconditioned response
13. shaping
14. cognitive
15. positive regard
16. humanistic-existential
17. humanistic-existential
18. sociocultural
19. positive
20. sociocultural

CHAPTER 3

RESEARCH IN ABNORMAL PSYCHOLOGY

CHAPTER OVERVIEW

Claims regarding treatments or explanations of behavior can be established only through systematic research. Each research method has its particular range of applications, its strengths, and its limitations.

The *case study* is a detailed account of one person's history, current circumstances, and psychological problems. It is often hoped that the case study will provide tentative support for a theory, but this method is weak in both *internal validity* and *external validity*. The case study can, however, challenge or refute a theoretical assumption, generate hypotheses for further research, suggest or demonstrate therapy techniques, and illustrate unusual or rare types of abnormality.

The *correlational method* is a procedure for evaluating whether two or more variables are related. The procedure requires that the variables of interest be measured in a sample of persons. The researcher then calculates a *correlation coefficient,* which provides a numerical index of the direction (positive or negative) and magnitude of the relationship. This index is typically tested to determine whether it is statistically significant (a reliable or dependable finding) or whether it is likely to have occurred by chance. Even though a significant correlation does not necessarily indicate a causal link, it can be useful to know that two variables are related.

An *experiment* tests a *hypothesis*. In its true form an experiment requires the manipulation of one variable, the *independent variable*, and the measurement of another, the *dependent variable*. *Confounds* are variables other than the independent variable that also act on the dependent variable. Experimenters seek to minimize their effects by the use of *control groups* and *experimental groups*, *random assignment*, and *blind designs*.

A true experiment in abnormal psychology is not always possible because of ethical or practical constraints. In these cases, researchers often rely on experimental designs that incorporate only some of the features of a true experiment. The *quasi-experimental design* and the *natural experiment* lack random assignment, and may be limited with respect to internal validity, but both may contribute important knowledge about abnormal psychology. The *analogue experiment* is an attempt to create a laboratory model of an abnormal behavior pattern and is a true experiment in the sense that it includes manipulation and random assignment. Consequently, it can be said to possess internal validity, but its external validity is uncertain. The *single-subject experiment* may take the form of an *ABAB design* or a *multiple-baseline design*. These experiments, too, have internal validity but their external validity appears to be limited.

The study of abnormality may be best served by the use of all of these methods. Different research questions often require different research methods. In the ideal situation, several independent researchers using various methods produce findings whose conclusions converge.

KEY TERMS

case study

internal validity

external validity

correlational method

experiment

hypothesis

independent variable

dependent variable

confounds

control group

experimental group

random assignment

blind design

quasi-experimental design

natural experiment

analogue experiment

single-subject experiment

ABAB design

multiple-baseline design

SAMPLE
MULTIPLE-CHOICE
QUESTIONS

1. Symptom substitution is an issue raised by proponents of which model of abnormality?
   a. behavioral
   b. cognitive
   c. psychodynamic
   d. humanistic-existential

2. A correlational study that finds that people who repeatedly experience life stresses are increasingly likely to become depressed indicates that life stress and depression are:
   a. positively correlated
   b. negatively correlated
   c. not related

3. Which research method is lacking in internal validity?
   a. correlational study
   b. experiment
   c. analogue experiment
   d. single-subject experiment

4. A longitudinal study is actually a special form of:
   a. experimental study
   b. analogue study
   c. correlational study
   d. case study

5. In an experiment, the manipulated variable is called the:
   a. control variable
   b. dependent variable
   c. independent variable
   d. correlated variable

6. Subject and experimenter bias in an experiment are typically controlled by:
   a. random assignment
   b. the Rosenthal method
   c. a control group
   d. a blind design

7.   The major concern with respect to analogue studies is that they:
     a. may lack internal validity
     b. may lack external validity
     c. are correlational studies
     d. lack a control group

8.   The ABAB design is a type of:
     a. analogue study
     b. quasi-experiment
     c. natural experiment
     d. single-subject experiment

9.   Single-subject designs require the experimenter to measure the subject's behavior:
     a. before a manipulation
     b. after a manipulation
     c. both a and b
     d. neither a nor b

10. A multiple-baseline design is a type of:
     a. natural experiment
     b. quasi-experiment
     c. analogue experiment
     d. single-subject experiment

SAMPLE SHORT-ANSWER QUESTIONS

1.   The nomothetic approach to understanding abnormal behavior is typically contrasted with the _____approach.

2.   A tentative explanation advanced to provide a basis for an investigation is called a(n)_____.

3.   The degree to which the findings of a study can be generalized beyond the study itself is called _____ validity.

4.   Research has found that the rate of schizophrenia and socioeconomic status are negatively correlated; that is, the rate of schizophrenia is _____ among groups of lower socioeconomic status than among groups of higher socioeconomic status.

23

5. The purpose of doing a statistical analysis of research data is to determine the likelihood that the findings will occur _____.

6. The number of new cases of a disorder that occur within a particular time interval is called the _____ of the disorder.

7. The total number of cases of a particular disorder in a population at a particular point in time is referred to as the _____ of the disorder.

8. Although correlational studies can describe the relationship between two variables, they cannot indicate _____.

9. The control group in an experiment is not exposed to the _____ variable.

10. An experiment can reduce confounds by selecting subjects for the experimental and control groups by _____.

11. Some quasi-experimental designs make use of _____ control groups.

12. Natural experiments are actually one type of _____ experiment.

13. The study of survivors of the dam disaster at Buffalo Creek, West Virginia, is a(n)_____ experiment.

14. The procedure used by Seligman to investigate learned helplessness is a(n) _____ experiment.

15. Seligman's learned helplessness study appears to have high_____ validity.

16. The logic of single-subject designs is that subjects serve as their own _____.

17. The ABAB design is also called a(n) _____ design.

18. Each "B" in the ABAB design represents the introduction of the_____ variable.

19. In single-subject designs, the observation period before the manipulation of an independent variable is called the
_____.

20. Single-subject designs are considered to be secure from the standpoint of _____ validity but to be weaker in _____ validity.

EXPLANATIONS OF DIFFICULT MATERIAL

An investigation is said to be *internally valid* (or to have *internal validity*) if the results can be attributed to the independent variable. *External validity*, on the other hand, is the degree to which conclusions can be generalized to settings or populations other than those specifically studied. Obviously, research findings must fulfill the requirements of internal validity and external validity if they are to be regarded as having scientific merit and relevance.

Each research method should be considered in the light of its internal and external validity. The case study method obviously lacks internal validity because several possible independent variables (other than the one identified by the reporter of the case study) could have caused the outcome or effect reported. Also, the case study lacks external validity because it deals with only a single case. Correlational studies lack internal validity because the two correlated variables may not be causally linked or the causation may be in the opposite direction from the one suspected. The method may have external validity in the sense that similar findings may well apply to other populations or situations. Provided that appropriate attention has been paid to such matters as control groups, random assignment, and experimenter and subject bias, the experimental method meets the test of internal validity, but the external validity of an experiment is often more difficult to discern.

The quasi-experimental design and the natural experiment are clearly compromises with respect to internal validity. The studies may possess external validity in the sense that similar findings may be made in other settings or other populations. The analogue experiment does have internal validity, provided that appropriate attention is paid to the basic elements of the scientific method. The quasi-experimental design and the natural experiment, by definition, do not have internal validity. The external validity of the analogue experiment is uncertain.

25

All research methods, despite their various limitations, can contribute to the advancement of the field of abnormal psychology. A research area or question often dictates the approach the researcher must take. Ideally, if a particular research question can be investigated by two or more methods, and if the findings obtained by the various methods essentially converge, confidence in the conclusions drawn from the research is strengthened.

ADDITIONAL READINGS

Agnew, N. McK., & Pyke, S. W. (1987). *The science game: An introduction to research in the social sciences* (4th ed.). Englewood Cliffs, N.J.: Prentice-Hall.

Bellack, A. S., & Herson, M. (Eds.). (1984). *Research methods in clinical psychology.* New York: Pergamon.

Cozby, P.C. (1989). *Methods in behavioral research* (4th ed.). Mountain View, CA: Mayfield.

Kazdin, A. E. (1980). *Research design in clinical psychology.* New York: Harper & Row.

Miller, N. E. (1985). The value of behavioral research on animals. *American Psychologist, 40,* 423–440.

Ray, W. J., & Ravizza, R. (1988). *Methods toward a science of behavior and experience* (3rd ed.). Belmont, Calif.: Wadsworth.

ANSWER KEY

Multiple-Choice Questions:

1c, 2a, 3a, 4c, 5c, 6d, 7b, 8d, 9c, 10d.

Short-Answer Questions:

1. idiographic
2. hypothesis
3. external
4. higher
5. by chance
6. incidence
7. prevalence
8. causation
9. independent (experimental) variable
10. random assignment

11. matched
12. quasi
13. natural
14. analogue
15. internal
16. controls
17. reversal
18. independent (or experimental or treatment)
19. baseline
20. internal, external

CHAPTER 4

CLINICAL ASSESSMENT, INTERPRETATION, AND DIAGNOSIS

CHAPTER OVERVIEW

The purposes of clinical *assessment* are to explain abnormal behavior, make a diagnosis, evaluate change, and aid research. Clinical assessment procedures include the clinical interview, clinical tests, and observational methods.

The *clinical interview* is the most widely used assessment procedure and is typically the first contact between a practitioner and a distressed person. Interviews may be either structured or unstructured.

The information gleaned from *clinical tests* supplements information obtained in other ways. To be useful, a test must meet the requirements of *standardization* (be administered to a large group of subjects whose performance then serves as a standard against which any score can be measured), *reliability* (consistency), and *validity*. Researchers administer *projective tests, personality inventories,* and other *self-report inventories, psychophysiological tests, neuropsychological tests,* and *intelligence tests.*

Naturalistic (in vivo) observations and *structured observations* provide information useful for clinical assessment. *Self-monitoring,* or subject's reporting on specific aspects of his or her own behavior, cognitions, or emotions, is also useful in some clinical situations. Observational techniques have their strengths and limitations in the clinical assessment process.

The final steps of the assessment process require the clinician to interpret the assessment data and formulate a clinical picture of the person, which usually includes a diagnosis. The diagnosis reflects a determination that the person's problems meet the criteria for a particular mental disorder. The classification system currently in use in the United States is the revised third edition of the American Psychiatric Association's *Diagnostic and Statistical Manual of Mental Disorders (DSM-III-R)*.

KEY TERMS

assessment

clinical interview

clinical test

standardization

reliability

validity

projective tests

personality inventories

self-report inventories

psychophysiological tests

neuropsychological tests

intelligence tests

naturalistic (in vivo) observations

structured observations

self-monitoring

DSM-III-R

SAMPLE MULTIPLE-CHOICE QUESTIONS

1. A functional analysis is part of:
   a. personality assessment
   b. DSM-III-R diagnosis
   c. behavioral assessment
   d. intellectual assessment

2. In the acronym SORC, which behavioral
    interviewers use to gather information relating to a
    functional analysis, the *R* stands for:
    a. reinforcement history
    b. abnormal responses
    c. reports of others
    d. personal resources

3. Alternate-form reliability for a test seems most similar
    to:
    a. test-retest reliability
    b. construct reliability
    c. interrater reliability
    d. external reliability

4. Projective tests are used primarily by clinicians of which
    perspective?
    a. psychodynamic
    b. humanistic
    c. behavioral
    d. cognitive

5. The Rorschach is which type of clinical test?
    a. neuropsychological test
    b. intelligence test
    c. projective test
    d. personality inventory

6. The MMPI scales were constructed by the method of
    criterion keying. This means that the method was:
    a. based on expert judgment
    b. based on common sense
    c. empirical
    d. all of the above

7. What are the two major categories of Axis II disorders?
    a. developmental and personality disorders
    b. developmental and adjustment disorders
    c. personality and sleep disorders
    d. personality and sexual disorders

8. Structured observation is a method of clinical
    assessment that is most likely to be used by:
    a. humanistic practitioners
    b. psychodynamic practitioners
    c. existential practitioners
    d. behavioral practitioners

9. A clinician who uses Rorschach responses to infer unconscious conflicts concerning responsibility is using assessment information as a:
   a. sample
   b. correlate
   c. sign
   d. none of the above

10. What type of reliability applies to classification?
    a. test-retest
    b. alternate form
    c. internal
    d. interrater

SAMPLE
SHORT-ANSWER
QUESTIONS

1. Clinical practitioners arrive at an understanding of a client through a combination of what three activities?

   _____

   _____

   _____

2. Unstructured interviews are likely to be favored by clinicians of which perspectives?

   _____

   _____

3. Structured interviews are likely to be favored by clinicians of which perspectives?

   _____

   _____

4. The use of an interview schedule is part of a(n) _____ interview.

5. When a new psychological test is developed, a typical procedure is to administer the test to a large number of people. This group of people is called the _____ sample.

6. The split-half method applies to _____ reliability.

7. Scholastic aptitude tests (as for medical school or law school) are expected to have what type of validity?

_____

8. The first phase of the Rorschach test is called the

_____.

9. The drawing of human figures is used as a projective personality test, and is sometimes also used to evaluate

_____.

10. What two response sets occur with the MMPI?

_____

_____

11. The Q-sort has been used especially by clinicians of which perspective?

_____

12. Name one construct that would be assessed by an affective inventory.

_____

13. The Reinforcement Survey Schedule is likely to be used by practitioners of which perspective?

_____

14. Organic impairment is evaluated by which type of psychological test? _____

15. Clinical observations are categorized as either _____ or _____.

16. Self-monitoring is an assessment procedure that is most likely to be used by proponents of which models of abnormality?

_____

_____

17. It has been found that during self-monitoring of cigarette smoking, smokers tend to smoke fewer cigarettes than they normally do. This phenomenon is called a(n) _____ effect.

18. Clinicians use assessment information to determine whether a person's problems meet the criteria for a particular _____.

19. A cluster of symptoms that commonly occur together is called a(n) _____.

20. If it is shown that most cases assigned to a particular category have a similar history and cause, the category can be said to have _____ validity.

EXPLANATIONS OF DIFFICULT MATERIAL

Both versions of the Minnesota Multiphasic Personality Inventory (MMPI and MMPI-2) were constructed by criterion keying, a special method for selecting items to be included in a test or scale.

Criterion keying requires the identification of a set (or number) of items to which a criterion group of people and a "normal" group from the general population have responded differently; that is, one group has answered yes or true while the other has answered no or false. The criterion group comprises people who exhibit the characteristic that the scale is intended to measure.

The normal group, of course, is necessary for the purpose of comparison. If the scale is intended to measure depression, the members of the criterion group must be evaluated to ascertain that they are in fact depressed, and the members of the normal group must be evaluated to ascertain that in fact they are *not* depressed. The initial pool of potentially useful items can be gathered from any source. These initial items are administered to all subjects in the two groups.

Certain statistical procedures then enable the test developer to determine which of the items elicited responses that differed to a statistically significant degree ($p < .05$) between the two groups of subjects. Those items that meet the requirements of the statistical analysis are then included in the scale intended to measure the characteristic exhibited by the criterion group—in this case, the depression scale. The importance of ascertaining that the people in the two groups are correctly classified is obvious.

Criterion keying is an empirical procedure, and some items selected may seem contrary to common sense. This method is more trustworthy than common sense or clinical judgment because it is based on the way people do in fact respond to the various items. The items selected are those that differentiate a particular criterion group from a normal or general population group.

ADDITIONAL READINGS

Anastasi, A. (1988). *Psychological testing* (6th ed.). New York: Macmillan.

Bellack, A. S., & Hersen, M. (Eds.). (1988). *Behavioral assessment: A practical handbook* (3rd ed.). New York: Pergamon.

Blashfield, R. K., & Livesley, W. J. (1991). Metaphorical analysis of psychiatric classification as a psychological test. *Journal of Abnormal Psychology, 100,* 262–270.

Kolb, B., & Whisaw, I. Q. (1990). *Fundamentals of neuropsychology* (3rd ed.). New York: W. H. Freeman.

McReynolds, P. (1989). Diagnosis and clinical assessment: Current status and major issues. In M. R. Rosenzweig & L. W. Porter (Eds.), *Annual review of psychology* (pp. 83–108). Palo Alto, Calif.: Annual Review.

Nietzel, M. T., Bernstein, D. A., & Milich, R. (1991). *Introduction to clinical psychology* (3rd ed.). Englewood Cliffs, N.J.: Prentice-Hall.

Phares, E. J. (1988). *Clinical psychology* (3rd ed.). Homewood, Ill.: Dorsey.

ANSWER KEY

Multiple-Choice Questions:

1c, 2b, 3a, 4a, 5c, 6c, 7a, 8d, 9c, 10d.

Short-Answer Questions:

1. assessment, interpretation, diagnosis
2. psychodynamic, humanistic
3. behavioral, cognitive, biological
4. structured
5. standardization
6. internal
7. predictive
8. free association phase
9. intelligence
10. acquiescence, social desirability
11. humanistic
12. depression (or anxiety or anger)

13. behavioral
14. neuropsychological
15. naturalistic, structured
16. behavioral, cognitive
17. reactivity
18. disorder
19. syndrome
20. etiological

CHAPTER 5

TREATMENTS FOR ABNORMAL PSYCHOLOGICAL FUNCTIONING

CHAPTER OVERVIEW

Psychotherapy is an interactive process in which the troubled person and the therapist engage jointly; *biological therapy* consists of physical and chemical procedures. A further distinction is made between systems and formats of therapy. A therapy *system* is the theoretical framework within which therapy is conducted; the *format* is determined by the way the therapy is applied: to an individual, group, family, or couple. Global therapies aim at changing general aspects of personality; specific therapies focus on the symptoms without consideration of more general aspects of personality.

A central assumption of the *psychodynamic therapies* is that inner conflicts resulting from past events must be identified, brought to the patient's awareness, and worked through so that the problem can be resolved. Key aspects of the psychodynamic system include *free association, resistance,* and *transference*. The therapist interprets the patient's dreams, translating the *manifest content* into the *latent content*. Ideally the patient experiences *catharsis*, or reliving of repressed feelings, and gains insight by the process of *working through*.

Client-centered therapy, a humanistic approach developed by Carl Rogers, emphasizes the crucial importance of the therapist-client relationship. If the therapist shows *unconditional positive regard, accurate empathy,* and *genuineness* (or *congruence*), the client will become more self-accepting—a process known as *experiencing*. *Gestalt therapy*, also a humanistic approach, is based on the belief that mental disorders result from distortions of *figure-ground relationships:* our needs stand out prominently in our lives, but when they are fulfilled they retreat into the background. The goal of gestalt therapy, like that of client-centered therapy, is self-awareness and self-acceptance, but gestalt therapists are much more active and directive. Among their techniques are *skillful frustration, role playing,* and *exercises and games.*

Existential therapy emphasizes the need to accept responsibility for one's life and to recognize one's freedom to choose an *authentic life.*

Behavioral therapies represent the application of principles of learning to the modification of abnormal behavior patterns. Among techniques based on classical conditioning are *systematic desensitization,* including construction of a *fear hierarchy,* and *aversion therapy. Token economy* programs are based on principles of operant conditioning. Modeling principles are followed in *social skills training.*

A central assumption of the *cognitive therapies* is that abnormal functioning is caused by maladaptive attitudes, beliefs, and thoughts. Albert Ellis's *rational-emotive therapy* aims to help clients recognize and change their irrational assumptions. Aaron Beck's *cognitive therapy* helps clients change their illogical thoughts into more adaptive ways of thinking. Among *cognitive-behavioral therapies* is *self-instruction training,* which teaches clients to make helpful *self-statements* in difficult situations.

Among the *biological therapies,* the most common is the use of *psychotropic drugs.* The *antianxiety drugs (minor tranquilizers or anxiolytics)* reduce tension but do not effect a cure. The *antidepressant drugs* include *monoamine oxidase (MAO) inhibitors* and *tricyclics. Antibipolar drugs* help stabilize moods. *Antipsychotic (neuroleptic) drugs* alleviate the confusion, hallucinations, and delusions of psychosis but can produce unwanted effects, the most serious of which are *extrapyramidal effects* and *tardive dyskinesia.* Other biological treatments are *electroconvulsive therapy (ECT),* which is used less frequently than drug therapy, and psychosurgery or *lobotomy,* which is seldom performed today.

Individual therapy is the oldest and most widely used format for therapy. Among group therapies are *psychodrama, encounter groups, T-groups,* and *self-help groups.*

Family therapy treats the family as a unit. Most family therapists adhere to *family systems theory. Structural family therapy* focuses mainly on the family power structure; *conjoint family therapy* emphasizes communication patterns. Marital or *couples therapy* also focuses on the structure and communication patterns in the couple's relationship. *Behavioral marital therapy* aims to help spouses recognize and change problem behaviors and reestablish *core symbols.*

Research findings indicate that psychotherapy is often effective and that the various therapies appear to be similar in overall effectiveness. Some approaches do appear to be particularly effective for certain disorders.

KEY TERMS

psychotherapy

biological therapy

free association

resistance

transference

manifest content

latent content

catharsis

working through

client-centered therapy

unconditional positive regard

accurate empathy

genuineness (congruence)

experiencing

gestalt therapy

figure-ground relationships

skillful frustration

role playing

exercises and games

authentic life

systematic desensitization

fear hierarchy

aversion therapy

token economy

social skills training

rational-emotive therapy

cognitive therapy

self-instruction training

self-statements

psychotropic drugs

antianxiety drugs (minor tranquilizers, anxiolytics)

antidepressant drugs

monoamine oxidase (MAO) inhibitors

tricyclics

antibipolar drugs

antipsychotic (neuroleptic) drugs

extrapyramidal effects

tardive dyskinesia

electroconvulsive therapy (ECT)

lobotomy

psychodrama

encounter groups

T-groups

self-help groups

family therapy

family systems theory

structural family therapy

conjoint family therapy

marital (couples) therapy

behavioral marital therapy

core symbols

SAMPLE MULTIPLE-CHOICE QUESTIONS

1. Which of the following are classified as global therapies?
    a. cognitive therapies
    b. behavioral therapies
    c. both a and b
    d. neither a nor b

2. According to Rogers, if the client is to make positive personality changes, the therapist must provide unconditional positive regard, accurate empathy, and:
    a. humor
    b. genuineness
    c. problem-solving ability
    d. support

3. The technique of role playing is most likely to be used in:
    a. psychodynamic therapy
    b. client-centered therapy
    c. gestalt therapy
    d. existential therapy

4. The form of therapy that is most likely to be effective with a person who wants to stop smoking cigarettes is:
    a. systematic desensitization
    b. aversion therapy
    c. social skills training
    d. client-centered therapy

5. A token economy is based mainly on principles of:
    a. operant conditioning
    b. classical conditioning
    c. modeling
    d. figure-and-ground

6. Minor tranquilizers (such as Valium) are effective for the treatment of:
    a. anxiety and tension
    b. schizophrenia
    c. overactive children
    d. aggressiveness

7. Which group of antidepressants may cause serious undesired effects if they are used in association with certain foods?
    a. tricyclics
    b. MAO inhibitors
    c. phenothiazines
    d. lithium

8. Tardive dyskinesia is an undesired effect of which of the following psychotropic drugs?
    a. antibipolar drugs
    b. antidepressant drugs
    c. antianxiety drugs
    d. antipsychotic drugs

9. The most effective of all therapies for the treatment of phobic disorders is:
    a. psychodynamic therapy
    b. client-centered therapy
    c. gestalt therapy
    d. behavior therapy

10. The "deterioration effect" refers to the fact that:
    a. some patients worsen during the course of therapy
    b. some patients worsen following a course of therapy
    c. patients often worsen initially in therapy and then improve
    d. none of the above

SAMPLE SHORT-ANSWER QUESTIONS

1. Individual, group, family, and marital are therapy _____.

2. Which three therapy systems are global therapies?
    _____
    _____
    _____

3. The development of insight is central to which therapy system? _____

4. According to the psychodynamic system, therapists interpret what three phenomena that occur during therapy?

   _____
   _____
   _____

5. The consciously remembered content of a dream is called its _____ content.

6. Is transference beneficial or harmful to psychodynamic therapy?

7. Is countertransference beneficial or harmful to psychodynamic therapy?

8. Resistance in therapy is an important construct for which therapy system? _____

9. Client-centered therapy was developed by _____.

10. In which therapy system is there a rule that clients use "I" language rather than "it" language?

    _____

11. A fear hierarchy is an important part of which therapy?

    _____

12. Social skills training is based on principles of _____.

13. Rational-emotive therapy is a type of _____ therapy.

14. Meichenbaum's self-instruction training teaches clients to modify their _____.

15. In the 1980s a new group of antidepressants was discovered. This group includes the highly regarded drug called _____.

16. The most effective of the antibipolar drugs is _____.

46

17. Research has shown that the most effective single form of treatment for schizophrenic disorders consists of _____.

18. ECT is used primarily with patients who have which disorder? _____

19. Role reversal is a part of which group therapy? _____

20. The term *homeostasis* is an important concept for which therapy approach? _____

EXPLANATIONS OF DIFFICULT MATERIAL

Clinicians and researchers in general agree that the condition of some clients seems to worsen over the course of treatment, and substantial data support the idea that therapy can have negative effects. Clearly, the factors that lead to deterioration effects require investigation.

Research has indicated similar overall success rates for various psychotherapy interventions (systems and formats), yet some therapies do seem to be more effective than others for specific disorders. The implication is that some therapies are *less* effective than others for particular disorders. Perhaps the inappropriate use of certain techniques or the use of a technique other than the treatment of choice will be found to contribute to the deterioration effect. Other factors that seem likely to contribute to negative outcomes are the characteristics of the client and the therapist. A client's lack of motivation to cooperate with the therapist, severe symptoms, and ineffective interpersonal relationships might lower the chances of a successful outcome.

A therapist's inability to communicate unconditional positive regard, empathy, and genuineness, similarly, might lead to a negative outcome. Finally, it seems possible that a particular therapist may simply be incompatible with a particular client. It is less important to identify all factors that might lead to deterioration effects than to recognize that these effects do have an explanation. It remains for clinicians and researchers to discover those factors that lead to a bad outcome.

ADDITIONAL READINGS

Berzins, J. I. (1977). Therapist-patient matching. In A. S. Gurman & A. M. Razin (Eds.), *Effective psychotherapy: A handbook of research.* New York: Pergamon.

Crits-Christoph, P., Cooper, P., & Luborsky, L. (1988). The accuracy of therapists' interpretations and the outcome of dynamic psychotherapy. *Journal of Consulting and Clinical Psychology, 56,* 490–495.

Dobson, K. S. (Ed.) (1988). *Handbook of cognitive-behavioral therapies.* New York: Guilford.

Freeman, A., Simon, K. M., Beutler, L. E., & Arkowitz, H. (Eds.) (1989). *Comprehensive handbook of cognitive therapy.* New York: Plenum.

Goldfried, M. R., Greenberg, L. S., & Marmar, C. (1990). Individual psychotherapy: Process and outcome. In M. R. Rosenzweig & L. W. Porter (Eds.), *Annual review of psychology* (pp. 659–688). Palo Alto, Calif.: Annual Review.

Hermalin, J. E., & Morell, J. A. (Eds.) (1987). *Prevention planning in mental health.* Newbury Park, Calif.: Sage.

Hollon, S., & Beck, A. T. (1986). *Handbook of psychotherapy and behavior change* (3rd ed.). New York: Wiley.

Kanfer, F. H., & Goldstein, A. P. (Eds.) (1991). *Helping people change: A textbook of methods.* (4th ed.). New York: Pergamon.

Valenstein, E. S. (1986). *Great and desperate cures.* New York: Basic Books.

ANSWER KEY

Multiple-Choice Questions:

1d, 2b, 3c, 4b, 5a, 6a, 7b, 8d, 9d, 10a.

Short-Answer Questions:

1. formats
2. psychodynamic, humanistic, existential
3. psychodynamic (psychoanalytic)
4. transference, resistance, dreams
5. manifest
6. beneficial
7. harmful
8. psychodynamic (psychoanalytic)

9. Carl Rogers
10. gestalt
11. systematic desensitization
12. modeling
13. cognitive
14. self-statements
15. Prozac
16. lithium
17. antipsychotic drugs
18. depression
19. psychodrama
20. family therapy

CHAPTER 6

ANXIETY DISORDERS

CHAPTER OVERVIEW

The predominant symptom of the *anxiety disorders* is a feeling of unspecified threat, or *anxiety*. The anxiety response is produced by the *autonomic nervous system (ANS)*, the network of nerves that connect the *central nervous system* to the body organs. The ANS nerve fibers that produce the physical changes experienced as anxiety are known as the *sympathetic nervous system*. The *parasympathetic nervous system* returns body functioning to normal. A person's general level of anxiety, or *trait anxiety,* is distinguished from *situation* or *state anxiety.*

DSM-III-R distinguishes three categories of *phobic disorders:* *agoraphobia,* or fear of going outside one's home alone; *social phobia*, or fear of public scrutiny; and *simple* or *specific phobias,* fear of other stimuli and situations. *Generalized anxiety disorders* involve chronic and pervasive feelings of anxiety about a variety of circumstances.

Freud distinguished *realistic anxiety, neurotic anxiety,* and *moral anxiety.* Rogers attributes anxiety disorders to the development of harsh self-standards, or *conditions of worth.* Existentialists believe that these disorders grow out of *existential anxiety.* Behaviorists attribute them to *classical conditioning, modeling, operant conditioning,* and *stimulus generalization.* Behaviorists support their explanations by

51

evidence of *vicarious conditioning* in the laboratory, and propose a theory of *preparedness* for some phobias. Cognitive explanations focus on *automatic thoughts.* *Concordance studies* support biological explanations.

Panic attacks are repeated episodes of intense fear with physical symptoms that come on suddenly. Research findings in the biological area have been especially promising in suggesting an explanation for *panic disorders.* Recently the proposal that biological and cognitive factors may combine to produce panic attacks has been advanced.

The essential features of the *obsessive compulsive disorder* include the occurrence of *obsessions,* repetitive and unwanted thoughts, and *compulsions,* repetitive and rigid activities that the individual feels driven to complete. When obsessions and compulsions become extreme, distressing, and handicapping, the behavior pattern is diagnosed as a disorder. Freud traced such disorders to suppression of *aggressive impulses.* Other psychodynamic theorists attribute them to three ego defense mechanisms: *isolation, undoing,* and *reaction formation.* Behaviorists focus on chance associations. The psychodynamic view lacks empirical support and the behavioral view considers only compulsions. Researchers have identified biological variables in these disorders but have not yet discovered the roles played by these variables.

The post-traumatic stress disorder (PTSD) is regarded as a reaction to an extreme stressor that is outside the range of normal experience. The symptoms include reexperiencing of the traumatic event by conscious recollections or dreams, an avoidance of associated situations, reduced responsiveness to the external world, and an increase in physiological arousal. The disorder may arise as a result of combat or other traumatic experiences. The symptoms are pronounced in the *rape trauma syndrome.* People armed with a set of positive attitudes, or *hardiness,* are less likely to develop symptoms of post-traumatic stress disorder.

KEY TERMS

anxiety disorders

anxiety

autonomic nervous system (ANS)

central nervous system

sympathetic nervous system

parasympathetic nervous system

trait anxiety

situation (state) anxiety

agoraphobia

social phobias

simple (specific) phobias

generalized anxiety disorders

realistic anxiety

neurotic anxiety

moral anxiety

conditions of worth

existential anxiety

classical conditioning

modeling

operant conditioning

stimulus generalization

vicarious conditioning

preparedness

automatic thoughts

concordance studies

panic attacks

panic disorders

obsessive compulsive disorders

obsessions

compulsions

aggressive id impulses

isolation

undoing

reaction formation

post-traumatic stress disorders

rape trauma syndrome

hardiness

SAMPLE
MULTIPLE-CHOICE
QUESTIONS

1. DSM-III-R distinguishes three types of phobias:
    agoraphobia, social phobia, and:
    a. animal phobia
    b. simple phobia
    c. situational phobia
    d. claustrophobia

2. Fear of scrutiny by others and of evaluation and
    humiliation are symptoms of:
    a. agoraphobia
    b. social phobia
    c. simple phobia
    d. all phobias

3. Free-floating anxiety is associated with:
    a. panic disorder
    b. obsessive compulsive disorder
    c. agoraphobia
    d. generalized anxiety disorder

4. Freud's case of Little Hans exemplifies the
    psychoanalytic view of the development of a(n):
    a. panic disorder
    b. generalized anxiety disorder
    c. phobic disorder
    d. obsessive compulsive disorder

5. If a phobia is learned on the basis of classical
    conditioning, the person's fear is the:
    a. conditioned stimulus
    b. conditioned response
    c. unconditioned stimulus
    d. unconditioned response

6. The study in which Little Albert was conditioned to fear
    white rats was:
    a. a case study
    b. a quasi-experiment
    c. an analogue study
    d. none of the above

7. Panic disorders are discrete episodes of symptoms that
    occur:
    a. in specific situations
    b. in response to a provoking stimulus
    c. at unpredictable times
    d. none of the above

8. Recent explanations of panic disorders that have
    received the most support combined:
    a. biological and cognitive perspectives
    b. biological and psychodynamic perspectives
    c. psychodynamic and behavioral perspectives
    d. existential and cognitive perspectives

9. Some researchers believe that panic attacks may be
    misinterpreted bodily sensations. This statement
    suggests a:
    a. behavioral explanation
    b. cognitive explanation
    c. psychodynamic explanation
    d. humanistic explanation

10. Obsessive compulsive disorders are classified as anxiety disorders because their victims experience great anxiety:
a. during the obsession or compulsion
b. after the obsession or compulsion
c. if they resist the obsession or compulsion
d. almost continuously

SAMPLE
SHORT-ANSWER
QUESTIONS

1. In earlier versions of the *Diagnostic and Statistical Manual*, anxiety disorders were called anxiety

_____.

2. What are the two parts of the autonomic nervous system?

_____

_____

3. A person's general level of anxiety is called _____ anxiety.

4. The majority of phobic disorders fall into which category?_____

5. Are phobic disorders and generalized anxiety disorders more common in men or in women?

_____

6. Of the five anxiety disorders described in Chapter 6, which two occur with the greatest frequency?

_____

_____

7. List the three types of anxiety proposed by Freud.

_____

_____

_____

8. According to Freudian theory, phobic individuals make excessive use of two defense mechanisms to control their underlying anxiety. What are these defense mechanisms?

_____

_____

9. According to Rogers, conditions of worth result when a person has failed to receive _____ as a child.

10. A fear may be acquired through observation and imitation. The technical term for this type of learning is _____.

11. Avoidance of a feared stimulus is an example of _____ conditioning.

12. Fear of a specific stimulus that becomes broadened so that other, similar stimuli also arouse the fear can be explained by the principle of _____.

13. DSM-III-R's criteria for panic disorder require the occurrence of four attacks within how long a time interval? _____

14. The class of psychotropic drugs that have been found to be effective in the treatment of panic disorders consists of _____.

15. The chemical named yohimbrine, which has induced panic attacks in humans, is assumed to produce its effect because it alters the activity of the neurotransmitter _____.

16. Some people with panic disorders have a cardiac malfunction called _____.

17. Obsessions are repetitive _____ and compulsions are repetitive _____.

18. Psychodynamic theorists view obsessive compulsive disorders as a battle between which two components of personality?

    _____

    _____

19. Behaviorists explain compulsions by proposing that they reduce _____.

20. Reexperiencing a traumatic event is one of the criteria for a diagnosis of _____.

EXPLANATIONS OF
DIFFICULT MATERIAL

One behavioral explanation of the development of phobias invokes the principles of classical conditioning to account for the acquisition of a fear of a particular stimulus and the learning of an avoidance response to the stimulus. Thus the conditioning explanation of phobias involves two stages, one based on classical conditioning and one based on operant conditioning.

Researchers have long sought to understand why phobias are so persistent. According to the classical conditioning paradigm, the phobic stimulus represents the conditioned stimulus (CS). The literature on classic conditioning makes it clear that the CS will extinguish if it is no longer paired with the unconditioned stimulus (US). Yet it is clear that phobias do not ordinarily extinguish. Can the behavioral model explain the apparent persistence of phobias? An extinction trial would require the phobic stimulus (CS) to be presented to the person without a following traumatic event (US). A person with a phobic disorder never experiences the CS without the US, and consequently the fear does not extinguish. Instead, the person with a phobia avoids the phobic stimulus, and avoidance is reinforced by reduction of the fear response. The reinforcement is automatic: every avoidance response represents an additional trial, which reduces fear and thus reinforces avoidance. This is the operant conditioning stage of the behavioral explanation of a phobia. This behavioral analysis makes the persistence of phobias understandable. Moreover, the necessary arrangements for the elimination of phobias by behavioral methods (which are described in Chapter 7) can already be anticipated.

ADDITIONAL READINGS

Jones, J. C., & Barlow, D. H. (1990). The etiology of post-traumatic stress disorder. *Clinical Psychology Review, 10,* 299–328.

Levin, A. P., Schneier, F. R., & Liebowitz, M. R. (1989). Social phobia: Biology and pharmacology. *Clinical Psychology Review, 9,* 129–140.

McNally, R. J. (1990). Psychological approaches to panic disorder: A review. *Psychological Bulletin, 108,* 403–419.

Rachman, S., & Bichard, S. (1988). The overprediction of fear. *Clinical Psychology Review, 8,* 303–312.

Warren, R., & Zgourides, G. D. (1991). *Anxiety disorders: A rational-emotive perspective.* Elmsford, N.Y.: Pergamon.

ANSWER KEY

Multiple-Choice Questions:

1b, 2b, 3d, 4c, 5b, 6a, 7c, 8a, 9b, 10c.

Short-Answer Questions:

1. neuroses
2. sympathetic, parasympathetic
3. trait
4. simple phobias
5. women
6. phobic disorders, generalized anxiety disorders
7. realistic, neurotic, moral
8. repression, displacement
9. unconditional positive regard
10. modeling (or vicarious conditioning)
11. operant
12. stimulus generalization
13. one month
14. antidepressant drugs
15. norepinephrine
16. mitral valve prolapse
17. thoughts (ideas, images), actions (activities)
18. id, ego
19. anxiety
20. post-traumatic stress disorder

CHAPTER 7

TREATMENTS FOR ANXIETY DISORDERS

CHAPTER OVERVIEW

In general, the psychodynamic, humanistic, and existential approaches to the treatment of anxiety disorders have had only modest success. Phobic, obsessive compulsive, and panic disorders seem to resist the global therapies.

The behavioral, cognitive, and biological approaches have made important contributions to the treatment of some of the anxiety disorders. Three behavioral approaches to the treatment of simple phobias, collectively known as *exposure-based treatments*, have had the most success. *Systematic desensitization*, developed by Joseph Wolpe on the principle of *reciprocal inhibition*, involves relaxation training and either *in vivo desensitization* or *covert desensitization*. *Flooding*, or *implosive therapy*, repeatedly exposes clients to the things they fear. Modeling techniques include *vicarious conditioning*; *participant modeling*, or *guided participation*; and *prolonged exposure*. The three approaches, while effective, are more effective if the procedure involves actual contact rather than imagined contact with the feared stimulus. The most significant benefit in the treatment of agoraphobia has come from in vivo exposure approaches. *Support groups* and *home-based self-help programs* have been developed to encourage victims of agoraphobia to confront the stimuli they fear and to reinforce successful efforts. People with social phobias seem to benefit from a variety of desensitization techniques, Ellis's *rational-emotive therapy*, and *social skills training*.

The generalized anxiety disorders are the least responsive to current treatments. The favored interventions are various cognitive therapies, including Beck's focus on *automatic thoughts;* stress management training, including *self-instruction training,* or *stress inoculation;* and *biofeedback* training, including the use of the *electromyograph (EMG)* and *electroencephalograph (EEG).* Antianxiety drugs have come to be used extensively in the treatment of anxious patients. They provide temporary relief in controlled doses but offer no long-term improvement.

Drug and cognitive therapies have had greater successes in the treatment of panic disorders. New understanding of the biological bases of panic disorders has followed from the discovery that people with these disorders can be helped by the antidepressant drugs. The relief obtained through the cognitive therapies seems to support the view that panic attacks may be caused in part by misinterpretation of physical sensations.

Obsessive compulsive disorders, once considered difficult to treat by any method, seem to yield somewhat to recent efforts. Viktor Frankl's *logotherapy* helps clients embrace the things that trouble them by the technique of *paradoxical intention.* Exposure and response prevention techniques have led to some successes in reducing or eliminating compulsive behavior patterns. Antidepressant drugs have also come to be recognized as helpful in the treatment of some obsessive compulsive disorders.

The treatment of the post-traumatic stress disorders has incorporated a combination of procedures. The specific techniques used are dictated by the nature of the symptoms and the complaints described by the client. Such a symptomatic focus is often supplemented by efforts to help the person gain an adaptive perspective on the traumatic event.

KEY TERMS

exposure-based treatments

systematic desensitization

reciprocal inhibition

in vivo desensitization

covert desensitization

flooding (implosive therapy)

vicarious conditioning

participant modeling (guided participation)

prolonged exposure

support groups

home-based self-help programs

rational-emotive therapy

social skills training

automatic thoughts

self-instruction training (stress inoculation)

biofeedback

electromyograph (EMG)

electroencephalograph (EEG)

logotherapy

paradoxical intention

exposure

response prevention

SAMPLE
MULTIPLE-CHOICE
QUESTIONS

1. Freud held that the treatment of the phobias required psychodynamic therapy:
   a. alone
   b. plus the therapist's encouragement
   c. plus the family's encouragement
   d. plus confrontation of the phobic stimulus

2. Clients treated by systematic desensitization are confronted by the objects or situations they fear:
   a. before a buzzer sounds
   b. while a buzzer is sounding
   c. while they are relaxed
   d. while they are eating a favorite food

3. Which of the following techniques is or are designed to reduce anxiety or fear?
   a. flooding
   b. implosive therapy
   c. both a and b
   d. neither a nor b

4. Do any of the following behavioral procedures appear to be superior in the treatment of phobias?
   a. actual exposure procedures
   b. imaginal exposure procedures
   c. both are equally effective
   d. both are equally ineffective

5. Ellis and Beck attempt to:
   a. help clients solve their own problems
   b. provide acceptance and support
   c. change maladaptive assumptions
   d. help clients be more assertive

6. The two antianxiety drugs most widely prescribed are:
   a. Valium and Librium
   b. Thorazine and Valium
   c. GABA and Parnate
   d. Librium and GABA

7. Antianxiety drugs are reported to be generally helpful for:
   a. generalized anxiety disorders
   b. panic disorders
   c. obsessive compulsive disorders
   d. all of the above

8. Most cognitive therapists consider that panic attacks are caused in part by:
   a. a feeling that one is not accepted by others
   b. a feeling that one is inferior
   c. misinterpretation of physical sensations
   d. misinterpretation of the reactions of others

9. Which anxiety disorders yield most readily to treatment?
   a. generalized anxiety disorders
   b. phobic disorders
   c. obsessive compulsive disorders
   d. dissociative disorders

10. The technique called paradoxical intention is used in:
    a. cognitive therapy
    b. logotherapy
    c. psychodynamic therapy
    d. client-centered therapy

SAMPLE
SHORT-ANSWER
QUESTIONS

1. The three exposure-based treatments used by behavioral therapists are:

   _____
   _____
   _____

2. Systematic desensitization was developed by

   _____.

3. The three phases of systematic desensitization are:

   _____
   _____
   _____

4. Systematic desensitization normally takes place in the imagination as the client visualizes the feared stimulus. When desensitization requires actual physical confrontation of the feared stimulus, it is called _____desensitization.

5. Vicarious conditioning is a form of _____.

6. Support groups have been developed to supplement exposure sessions in the treatment of which anxiety disorder?

    _____

7. When Albert Ellis treats people who have social phobias, he points out their _____.

8. Self-instructional training is based on techniques from which two therapy models?

    _____

    _____

9. People who are connected to a device that provides continuous information about certain physiological activities (such as blood pressure) are engaging in

    _____.

10. Before the 1950s, the drugs most often used to treat anxiety disorders were _____.

11. The first of the new antianxiety medications (meprobamate, Miltown) was discovered while efforts were being made to develop a more effective

    _____.

12. Which group of antianxiety drugs have become the most popular?_____.

13. List three drawbacks of the antianxiety drugs.

    _____

    _____

    _____

14. Panic attacks may be related to abnormal activity of the neurotransmitter substance _____.

15. The two most effective therapies for panic disorders are:

    _____

    _____

16. A behavioral technique developed to treat compulsive behavior is called

_____.

17. A cognitive-behavioral technique often used to treat clients who are troubled by obsessions is called

_____.

18. Which class of drugs has been found to be effective in obsessive compulsive disorders?

_____

19. The two anxiety disorders most recently recognized are:

_____

_____

20. A form of group therapy devised for patients with post-traumatic stress disorder is sometimes said to consist of

_____.

EXPLANATIONS OF
DIFFICULT MATERIAL

Clients with obsessive compulsive disorders who are exposed to the technique of paradoxical intention are urged to continue or exaggerate or increase the problem behavior. A client who feels compelled to wash her hands twenty times a day is urged to wash them even more frequently. A client who has the problem of obsessive thinking is urged to concentrate on nothing but his obsessions. Paradoxical intention has also been used to treat phobias. A person who suffers from agoraphobia is encouraged to go alone into stores and try to become anxious. This procedure seems to violate traditional ideas on how to bring about change in therapy. Yet clinical evidence, at least, does suggest that this procedure is beneficial to some clients.

Why does this "paradoxical" encouragement of the problem behavior actually result in its elimination? A behaviorist might say that requiring the client to produce the symptom is, in effect, making the symptom available for extinction. When the client is continuously and intensely engaged with the phobic stimulus, whether in vivo or through imaginal productions, these actions represent exposure and extinction. Another explanation that has been offered is that clients may come to view their symptom as under their conscious control. If the behavior can be performed more frequently, as the person has now done, it seems possible that it can also be performed less frequently. Several hypotheses have been offered to explain paradoxical intention as a therapy procedure. None of them has won universal acceptance nor is it clear when paradoxical intention is an appropriate technique to use.

ADDITIONAL READINGS

Barlow, D. H., Craska, M. G., Cerny, J. A., & Klosko, J. S. (1989). Behavioral treatment of panic disorders. *Behavior Therapy, 15,* 431–449.

Borden, J. W., Clum, G. A., & Salmon, P. G. (1991). Mechanisms of change in the treatment of panic disorders. *Cognitive Therapy and Research, 15,* 257–272.

Emmelkamp, P. M. G., Visser, S., & Hoekstra, R. J. (1988). Cognitive therapy vs. exposure in vivo in the treatment of obsessive compulsives. *Cognitive Therapy and Research, 12,* 103–114.

Lader, M. H. (1984). Antianxiety drugs. In T. B. Karasu (Ed.), *The psychiatric therapies.* Washington, D.C.: American Psychiatric Association.

Marks, I. M. (1983). Are there anticompulsive or antiphobic drugs? Review of the evidence. *British Journal of Psychiatry, 143,* 338–347.

Mattick, R. P., Petters, L., & Clarke, J. C. (1989). Exposure and cognitive restructuring for social phobia: A controlled study. *Behavior Therapy, 20,* 3–24.

Williams, S. L., & Rappoport, A. (1983). Cognitive treatment in the natural environment for agoraphobics. *Behavior Therapy, 14,* 299–313.

ANSWER KEY

Multiple-Choice Questions:

1d, 2c, 3c, 4a, 5c, 6a, 7a, 8c, 9b, 10b.

Short-Answer Questions:

1. desensitization, flooding, modeling
2. Joseph Wolpe
3. relaxation training, construction of a fear hierarchy, graded pairing
4. in vivo
5. modeling
6. agoraphobia
7. irrational assumptions

8. cognitive, behavioral
9. biofeedback training
10. barbiturates
11. antibiotic
12. benzodiazepines
13. they offer no long-term solution; they are addictive; they are toxic if used with alcohol
14. norepinephrine
15. antidepressant drugs, cognitive therapy
16. exposure and response prevention
17. thought stopping
18. antidepressant drugs
19. post-traumatic stress disorder, panic disorder
20. rap groups

CHAPTER 8

MOOD DISORDERS

CHAPTER OVERVIEW

Extreme fluctuations in mood from *depression* to *mania* are the predominant features and defining characteristics of the mood disorders. Most people who are diagnosed as having a mood disorder experience only depression, a pattern called *unipolar depression*. A pattern in which periods of mania alternate with periods of depression is called *bipolar* or *manic-depressive disorder*. People with depressive disorders exhibit emotional, motivational, behavioral, cognitive, and somatic symptoms. A severely disabling depression characterized by five or more symptoms and lasting at least 2 weeks is considered to be a *major depressive episode*. A less disabling depression with fewer symptoms is diagnosed as *dysthymia*. When dysthymia leads to a major depression, the sequence is called *double depression*. Some depressed people experience *delusions* and *hallucinations*. Clinicians no longer distinguish between *reactive depression* and *endogenous depression*; they now recognize both external and internal factors in the disorder.

Psychodynamic theory views depression as inward-directed anger, the final step in a sequence of unconscious processes that follow from a real or imagined loss. Children separated from their mothers before the age of 6 become passive and slow to develop, in a pattern called *anaclitic depression*.

A behavioral view proposed by Peter Lewinsohn hypothesizes a link between a reduction in positive reinforcement and the onset of depression. Beck attributes depression to the *cognitive triad:* negative *automatic thoughts* about one's experiences, oneself, and the future.

Another psychological view of depression regards a perception of loss of control over reinforcements as leading to *learned helplessness* and depression. The revised learned helplessness theory incorporates the attributions of people concerning their perceived lack of control.

Family pedigree studies, twin studies, and adoption studies make it clear that unipolar depression has a genetic component. The *catecholamine theory* traces unipolar depression to a low level of the neurotransmitter norepinephrine; the *indoleamine theory* attributes it to a deficiency of serotonin.

Manic episodes are periods of dramatic and inappropriate elation. People who experience such episodes receive diagnoses of *bipolar disorder, mixed,* if mania alternates rapidly with depression; *bipolar disorder, depressed,* if only depressive symptoms are currently presented; or *bipolar disorder, manic* if only manic symptoms are currently presented. Mood swings between milder depressive and *hypomanic* episodes are diagnosed as *cyclothymia.* Progress in understanding the bipolar disorders has been made only during the last half of this century, by biological researchers. Norepinephrine and serotonin, the neurotransmitters implicated in unipolar depression, have been implicated in manic states also. An imbalance in sodium ions in the neurons has also been found to be a factor in bipolar disorders, and *genetic linkage studies* have found evidence of genetic factors in these disorders.

KEY TERMS

depression

mania

unipolar depression

bipolar (manic-depressive) disorder

major depressive episode

dysthymia

double depression

delusions

hallucinations

reactive depression

endogenous depression

anaclitic depression

cognitive triad

automatic thoughts

learned helplessness

family pedigree studies

proband

twin studies

adoption studies

catecholamine theory

indoleamine theory

manic episodes

bipolar disorder, mixed

bipolar disorder, depressed

bipolar disorder, manic

hypomanic episodes

cyclothymia

genetic linkage studies

SAMPLE MULTIPLE-CHOICE QUESTIONS

1. Bipolar disorders were once called:
   a. dysthymic disorders
   b. cyclothymic disorders
   c. manic-depressive disorders
   d. melancholia

2. The term used in DSM-III-R for the milder form of depressive disorder is:
   a. dysthymic disorder
   b. reactive depression
   c. endogenous depression
   d. melancholia

3. The psychodynamic theory of depression developed by Freud and Abraham proposed a similarity between clinical depression and:
   a. helplessness
   b. grief reaction
   c. chronic illness
   d. suffering

4. The behavior pattern of infants separated from their mothers is called:
   a. reactive depression
   b. endogenous depression
   c. grief reaction
   d. anaclitic depression

5. A limitation of Lewinsohn's research is that:
   a. most of the research involves animal studies
   b. depressed patients have not been included
   c. the studies are correlational
   d. only case studies are reported

6. The idea of the cognitive triad is associated with:
   a. Beck's theory of depression
   b. the learned helplessness theory of depression
   c. the symptoms of depression
   d. the sociocultural view of depression

7. According to the revised learned helplessness theory, people are more likely to experience helplessness and depression if they attribute their present lack of control to:
   a. external and unstable factors
   b. external and stable factors
   c. internal and unstable factors
   d. internal and stable factors

8. The two neurotransmitters that have been most frequently associated with unipolar depression are:
   a. reserpine and serotonin
   b. norepinephrine and serotonin
   c. reserpine and acetylcholine
   d. acetylcholine and norepinephrine

9. A person who is experiencing a depressive episode and has a past history of mania will receive a diagnosis of:
   a. bipolar disorder, depressed
   b. bipolar disorder, mixed
   c. bipolar disorder, dysthymia
   d. bipolar disorder, manic

10. Studies indicate that levels of norepinephrine in manic patients:
    a. are the same as those found in depressed patients
    b. are higher than those found in depressed patients
    c. are lower than those found in depressed patients
    d. show extreme variation within a single day

SAMPLE
SHORT-ANSWER
QUESTIONS

1. Is the incidence of depression higher in men or in women?

   _____

2. The symptoms of depression are seen in five areas of functioning:

    _____
    _____
    _____
    _____
    _____

3. When dysthymia leads to a major depression, it is sometimes referred to as

    _____.

4. To explain the fact that people often become depressed without losing a loved one, Freud proposed the idea of

    _____.

5. Psychoanalytic theorists view depression as fixation at the _____ stage of development.

6. In Lewinsohn's behavioral view, depression is associated with a decrease in _____.

7. The cognitive triad consists of negative feelings about

    _____, _____, and

    _____.

8. In the traditional view of depression, which of the symptom areas—emotional, motivational, behavioral, cognitive, or somatic—is primary? _____

9. Which of the symptom areas does Beck view as primary?

    _____

10. Seligman's theory of depression evolved initially from conditioning studies with _____ as subjects.

11. Researchers have used inescapable shock or noise to produce _____.

12. Research has shown that learned helplessness reactions can be prevented if subjects are first provided with experiences in which they do have control over

    _____.

13. The person who is the focus of a genetic study is called the _____.

14. The blood pressure drug reserpine, which causes depression in some people, lowers the level of the neurotransmitter _____.

15. The tricyclic antidepressant drugs increase the level of the neurotransmitter _____.

16. Most bipolar disorders begin with a _____ episode.

17. Mood disorders with mild depressive episodes and mild manic episodes are called _____ disorders.

18. Given the expected relationship between mania and norepinephrine, would one predict that the drug reserpine might reduce or worsen manic symptoms?
   _____

19. One effect of lithium is to _____ norepinephrine activity.

20. Do twin studies indicate a stronger genetic influence in unipolar depression or in the bipolar disorders?
   _____

EXPLANATIONS OF DIFFICULT MATERIAL

The major tenet of Peter Lewinsohn's explanation of unipolar depression is that depression follows from a reduction in positive reinforcement from the environment. The amount of positive reinforcement is in turn determined by the number and range of events that the person finds reinforcing, how available these reinforcers are in the environment, and how skillful the person is in obtaining them.

It can be enlightening to consider how changes in a person's environment can be conceptualized in terms of a reduction of positive reinforcement. People who retire from a job or lose a job may find that they lose satisfying relationships with co-workers. This experience can be seen to represent a reduction in positive reinforcement. If one's spouse or another close family member dies or if a relationship is terminated for some other reason, this loss, too, reduces positive reinforcement. People who are relatively isolated and who therefore depend on only one or two sources of reinforcement are especially vulnerable to circumstances that reduce reinforcement.

Moreover, this situation may lead to a classic vicious circle: reduction of positive reinforcement is followed by depression, withdrawal, and a reduction of activity, which further reduces positive reinforcement, which leads to deeper depression.

The amount of positive reinforcement one receives is also heavily influenced by one's social skills. People whose social skills are well developed are reinforced more frequently and more generously by more people than those who are socially awkward and shy. In fact, a person who lacks social skills is not reinforcing others for social interaction, and eventually other people are likely to stop interacting with that person. And such experiences reduce positive reinforcement.

ADDITIONAL READINGS

Abramson, L. Y., Metalsky, G. I., & Alloy, L. B. (1989). Hopelessness depression: A theory-based subtype of depression. *Psychological Review, 96,* 358–372.

Ahrens, A. H., & Abramson, L. Y. (1991). Changes in personal standards and dysphoria: A longitudinal approach. *Cognitive Therapy and Research, 15,* 47–68.

Barnett, P. A., & Gotlib, I. H. (1990). Cognitive vulnerability to depressive symptoms among men and women. *Cognitive Therapy and Research, 14,* 47–61.

Haaga, D. A. F., Dyck, M. J., & Ernst, D. (1991). Empirical status of cognitive theory of depression. *Psychological Bulletin, 110,* 215–236.

Lewinsohn, P. M., Duncan, E. M., Stanton, A. K., & Hautzinger, M. (1986). Age at first onset for nonbipolar depression. *Journal of Abnormal Psychology, 95,* 378–383.

Miranda, J., Persons, J. B., & Byers, C. N. (1990). Endorsement of dysfunctional beliefs depends on current mood state. *Journal of Abnormal Psychology, 99,* 237–241.

Robins, C. J., Block, P., & Peselow, E. D. (1990). Cognition and life events in major depressions: A test of the mediation and interaction hypotheses. *Cognitive Theory and Research, 14,* 299–313.

Sorenson, S. B., Rutter, C. M., & Aneshensel, C. S. (1991). Depression in the community: An investigation into age of onset. *Journal of Consulting and Clinical Psychology, 59,* 541–546.

ANSWER KEY

Multiple-Choice Questions:

1c, 2a, 3b, 4d, 5c, 6a, 7d, 8b, 9a, 10b.

Short-Answer Questions:

1. women
2. emotional, motivational, behavioral, cognitive, somatic
3. double depression
4. imagined or symbolic loss
5. oral
6. positive reinforcement
7. one's experiences, oneself, the future
8. emotional
9. cognitive
10. dogs
11. learned helplessness
12. reinforcements
13. proband
14. norepinephrine
15. norepinephrine
16. manic
17. cyclothymic
18. reduce
19. reduce
20. bipolar disorders

CHAPTER 9

TREATMENTS FOR MOOD DISORDERS

CHAPTER OVERVIEW

A wide range of treatments, from global to specific, have been used for unipolar depression. Psychodynamic therapists focus on the actual or imagined loss, with the accompanying dependence, that they assume to be the basis for the depression. Lewinsohn bases his approach on the theory that depression flows from a low level of positive reinforcement. His therapy therefore consists of efforts to increase positive reinforcement in the client's life. A group technique called *personal effectiveness training* gives group members opportunities to practice social skills. *Interpersonal psychotherapy (IPT)* focuses on various interpersonal aspects of a person's life. IPT therapists use the concepts and techniques of various therapy models to deal with the relevant interpersonal areas of the client's life. Beck's cognitive view of depression leads directly to the therapy task of examining and invalidating automatic thoughts, identifying distorted thinking and negative biases, and altering attitudes.

Electroconvulsive therapy (ECT) is one of the most controversial therapies for depression. *Bilateral ECT,* the conventional method, is increasingly being replaced by *unilateral ECT,* but the use of both methods has declined since the introduction of the antidepressant drugs. The major classes of such drugs are the *tricyclic antidepressants* and the *monoamine oxidase (MAO) inhibitors.* The tricyclics are generally more effective and have fewer dangerous unwanted effects than the MAO inhibitors.

The interpersonal, cognitive, and biological therapies for unipolar depression appear to be the most effective of the current approaches, and they are essentially of equal effectiveness, though research suggests that cognitive therapy may be more effective in preventing relapses.

With the introduction of *lithium* treatment, the prognosis for bipolar disorders has become more optimistic than it once was. Lithium not only reduces manic behavior but appears to be a *prophylactic drug*—one that helps prevent symptoms from developing. Many clinicians now favor use of concurrent psychotherapy to enhance the overall effectiveness of lithium therapy for bipolar disorders.

KEY TERMS

personal effectiveness training

interpersonal psychotherapy (IPT)

bilateral ECT

unilateral ECT

tricyclic antidepressants

monoamine oxidase (MAO) inhibitor

lithium

prophylactic drug

SAMPLE MULTIPLE-CHOICE QUESTIONS

1. Which of the following is most likely to be a concern of psychodynamic therapists in working with clients with unipolar depression?
   a. childhood physical abuse
   b. Oedipal (Electra) conflicts
   c. real or imagined losses
   d. all are about equally likely

2. Lewinsohn assumes that encouraging a depressed client to participate in activities will result in a more positive mood because of:
   a. distraction
   b. reinforcement
   c. both a and b
   d. neither a nor b

3. Personal effectiveness training is a procedure used in:
   a. psychodynamic therapy
   b. behavioral therapy
   c. cognitive therapy
   d. existential therapy

4. The effectiveness of interpersonal psychotherapy:
   a. has not been adequately evaluated
   b. is not supported by research findings
   c. is generally supported by research findings

5. The interpersonal psychotherapy model might use:
   a. psychodynamic procedures
   b. behavioral procedures
   c. humanistic procedures
   d. all of the above

6. Reattribution techniques are most likely to be useful for therapists who follow the:
   a. psychodynamic model
   b. behavioral model
   c. interpersonal psychotherapy model
   d. cognitive model

7. Contingency management is a procedure used in:
   a. psychodynamic therapy
   b. behavioral therapy
   c. interpersonal psychotherapy
   d. cognitive therapy

8. Tricyclic antidepressants are more frequently prescribed than monoamine oxidase inhibitors because:
   a. they are generally more effective
   b. they have less dangerous unwanted effects
   c. both a and b
   d. neither a nor b

9. What conclusion is warranted with respect to the relative effectiveness of cognitive, interpersonal, and biological therapies for mild to severe depression?
   a. biological therapy is superior
   b. cognitive and interpersonal therapies are superior
   c. interpersonal therapy is superior
   d. all are of essentially equal effectiveness

10. Lithium has been found to be effective for:
    a. treating manic episodes
    b. treating depressive episodes of bipolar disorders
    c. preventing manic episodes of bipolar patients
    d. all of the above

SAMPLE
SHORT-ANSWER
QUESTIONS

1. Psychodynamic therapists regard depressed clients as being extremely dependent. For this reason, they believe that a sensitive issue in therapy is the _____ phenomenon.

2. Lewinsohn's purpose in having the client fill out a Pleasant Events Schedule is to learn which activities are _____.

3. The systematic ignoring of a client's depressive behavior and attending to positive (nondepressive) behavior is referred to as _____.

4. The teaching of social skills can be interpreted as a means of increasing _____.

5. Lewinsohn's behavioral therapy program seems to be least helpful to clients who show a _____ degree of depression.

6. Interpersonal psychotherapy uses concepts from which three psychotherapy models?

    _____
    _____
    _____

7. What four interpersonal problem areas are identified by IPT therapists as requiring exploration?

    _____
    _____
    _____
    _____

8. What two names are associated with cognitive therapy?

    _____
    _____

9. Beck's therapy approach attempts to get clients to increase their activities, but he believes that the increase in activity must be followed by _____ interventions.

10. If cognitive therapists were to assign clients homework, the clients might be asked to record _____.

11. Research on cognitive therapy has shown that improvements in depression are correlated with improvements in _____.

12. Electroconvulsive therapy is regarded as the most effective intervention for _____.

13. The major common undesirable effect of electroconvulsive therapy is _____.

14. The discovery of monoamine oxidase inhibitors was accidental in that researchers were looking for a treatment for _____.

15. The first monoamine oxidase inhibitor developed was _____.

16. People who take MAO inhibitors for depression must watch their _____.

17. Antidepressant drugs are thought to alleviate depression because they increase the availability of two neurotransmitters:_____ and _____.

18. Comparisons of ECT and antidepressants generally find that which approach alleviates depression more rapidly? _____.

19. The treatment of choice for bipolar disorders is _____.

20. Many of the classes of drugs used in the treatment of mood disorders were discovered by _____.

EXPLANATIONS OF DIFFICULT MATERIAL

From the standpoint of evaluation, one distinct advantage of cognitive therapy for unipolar depression is that distorted cognitions can be assessed before a course of therapy and again after therapy, so that the degree to which they have been modified by therapy can be determined. It is then possible to determine if there is a relationship between improvement in depression and improvement in cognitive distortions, negative biases, and maladaptive attitudes. The primary task of the cognitive therapist is to identify and modify distorted thinking.

The therapist's success in achieving this major objective can be assessed by an irrational beliefs inventory. Clients who show little or no change on this dimension are likely to show minimal improvement in depression; clients who show considerable change are expected to show much greater improvement in depression also. This pattern has emerged from the minimal research that has explored this important question. It seems reasonable to expect that those clients who show the greatest improvement in cognitive functioning will also be less likely to suffer a relapse after their recovery.

ADDITIONAL READINGS

Beckham, E. E. (1990). Psychotherapy of depression research at a crossroads: Directions for the 1990s. *Clinical Psychology Review, 10,* 207–228.

Belsher, G., & Costello, C. G. (1988). Relapse after recovery from unipolar depression: A critical review. *Psychological Bulletin, 104,* 84–96.

Dobson, K. S. (1989). A meta-analysis of the efficacy of cognitive therapy for depression. *Journal of Consulting and Clinical Psychology, 57,* 414–419.

Holden, C. (1985). A guarded endorsement for shock therapy. *Science, 228,* 1510–1511.

Hollon, S. D., Shelton, R. C., & Loosen, P. T. (1991). Cognitive therapy and pharmacotherapy for depression. *Journal of Consulting and Clinical Psychology, 59,* 88–99.

Robinson, L. A., Berman, J. S., & Neimeyer, R. A. (1990). Psychotherapy for the treatment of depression: A comprehensive review of controlled outcome research. *Psychological Bulletin, 108,* 30–49.

Rush, A. J. (Ed.) (1982). *Short-term psychotherapies for depression: Behavioral, interpersonal, cognitive, and psychodynamic approaches.* New York: Guilford.

ANSWER KEY

Multiple-Choice Questions:

1c, 2b, 3b, 4c, 5d, 6d, 7b, 8c, 9d, 10d.

Short-Answer Questions:

1. transference
2. reinforcing
3. contingency management
4. positive reinforcement
5. severe
6. psychodynamic, behavioral, humanistic
7. grief reaction, interpersonal role dispute, interpersonal role transition, interpersonal deficits
8. Beck, Ellis
9. cognitive
10. thoughts
11. cognitive functioning
12. severe unipolar depressions
13. memory loss
14. tuberculosis
15. iproniazid
16. diet
17. norepinephrine, serotonin
18. ECT
19. lithium
20. accident

CHAPTER 10

SUICIDE

CHAPTER OVERVIEW

Suicide accounts for nearly 2 percent of deaths in the United States, and far more people, called *parasuicides,* make unsuccessful attempts to kill themselves. Suicide is defined as an intentioned death, but the circumstances surrounding some deaths make it difficult to know whether or not they were intentioned. Edwin Shneidman distinguishes four kinds of people who intentionally end their lives: *death seekers, death initiators, death ignorers,* and *death darers.* He also recognizes *subintentioned death*—a death in which the person has played an indirect or unconscious role. Karl Menninger's category of *chronic suicide* consists of people who behave in life-threatening ways over an extended period, but their intentions are not clear.

Researchers investigate suicide by conducting a *retrospective analysis* of the life of a person immediately before suicide and by studying people who survive a suicide attempt. Suicide is more common among people of lukewarm religious faith than among the devout; among men than among women; among the divorced, widowed, and single than among the married; and among whites than among minority groups with the exception of Native Americans, who have the highest suicide rate of all Americans.

Research on suicide has identified several factors that seem to increase the risk of suicide: stressful events and situations, such as serious illness, abusive environment, occupational stress, and role conflict; mood and thought changes, particularly *hopelessness* and *dichotomous thinking;* alcohol use; mental disorders; and modeling or imitation effects. Though these factors have been shown to be associated with suicide, it should be noted that most people who experience them never attempt suicide.

Psychodynamic theorists view suicide as hostility turned inward. Biological theorists look for a genetic component. Emile Durkheim, the foremost proponent of the sociocultural view, focused on the social context of suicide and distinguished *egoistic suicide,* committed by people who reject the structure of their society; *altruistic suicide,* committed by people who are well integrated in the social structure; and *anomic suicide,* committed by people whose society provides no adequate structure.

Suicide among children is not frequent but has increased in recent years, and even among normal children thoughts of suicide are not uncommon. Suicide rates rise sharply among teenagers and college students and are linked to depression, stress, and anger. Suicide rates are highest among the elderly, who are particularly vulnerable to illness, loss of friends and family members, loss of control over their lives, and loss of status.

Treatment for individuals who have attempted suicide typically focuses on the development of more constructive ways of handling stress and solving problems. Suicide prevention programs have been developed to help suicidal people assess their situations more accurately and act constructively. Such counselors are usually *paraprofessionals* who work under the supervision of a mental health professional. Although much has been learned about suicide in recent years, much remains unknown about why certain people take their own lives or attempt to do so.

KEY TERMS

parasuicide

death seekers

death initiators

death ignorers

death darers

subintentioned death

chronic suicide

retrospective analysis

hopelessness

dichotomous thinking

egoistic suicide

altruistic suicide

anomic suicide

paraprofessionals

SAMPLE MULTIPLE-CHOICE QUESTIONS

1. Shneidman distinguished four types of people who intend to take their lives. In which of the four is the intent to die most ambiguous?
    a. death seekers
    b. death initiators
    c. death ignorers
    d. death darers

2. Many child suicides fall into which of Shneidman's categories?
    a. death seekers
    b. death initiators
    c. death ignorers
    d. death darers

3. Which of the following groups has the lowest suicide rate?
   a. married
   b. single
   c. widowed
   d. divorced

4. Statistics reveal that:
   a. more men than women both attempt and carry out suicide
   b. more men than women commit suicide; more women than men attempt suicide
   c. more men than women attempt suicide; more women than men commit suicide
   d. more women than men both attempt and carry out suicide

5. Research has shown that the number of recent undesirable events in subjects' lives is highest among:
   a. suicide attempters
   b. nonsuicidal depressed patients
   c. nondepressed psychiatric patients
   d. all three groups

6. Women in professional positions have the highest suicide rate among women in the work force. This high rate may be attributable to:
   a. occupational stress
   b. role conflict
   c. both a and b
   d. neither a nor b

7. The suicide rate is highest among people with:
   a. mood disorders
   b. substance use disorders
   c. schizophrenia
   d. panic disorders

8. The psychodynamic view of suicide is that it develops from depression and:
   a. a longing for support
   b. self-directed anger
   c. fear of responsibility
   d. feelings of uncertainty

9. According to Durkheim's theory of suicide, the suicidal person who is isolated and alienated from society fits which category?
   a. anomic suicide
   b. altruistic suicide
   c. egoistic suicide
   d. hostile-aggressive suicide

10. With increasing age, the suicide rate:
   a. rises
   b. falls
   c. stays about the same
   d. rises to about age 40 or 50 and then declines

SAMPLE
SHORT-ANSWER
QUESTIONS

1. People who make unsuccessful attempts to kill themselves are referred to as _____.

2. Shneidman defines suicide as a(n)_____ death.

3. Shneidman considers the behavior of people who behave in life-endangering ways, as by mismanaging medications or engaging in high-risk occupations, to fit the category of _____.

4. The collection and investigation of information about the experiences and mental state of a person over the last few days before a suicide is called a(n)_____.

5. The highest suicide rate is found among people of which marital status?_____.

6. Is the suicide rate higher among whites or among blacks?
   _____

7. Some clinicians believe that the most sensitive indicator of suicidal intent is a feeling of
   _____.

8. What three mental disorders are linked most strongly to suicide?

   _____

   _____

   _____

9. A tendency to attempt suicide after news is spread about other suicides is called a(n)

   _____ effect.

10. Freud hypothesized that humans have a death instinct, which he called _____.

11. People who commit suicide appear to have lower levels of the neurotransmitter _____.

12. List the three categories of suicide described by Durkheim.

    _____

    _____

    _____

13. Durkheim's theory of suicide emphasizes the importance of _____ factors.

14. People in which age group, the elderly or teenagers, are more ambivalent about suicide?

15. Is the suicide rate for college students higher or lower than the rate for noncollege persons of the same age range?

    _____

16. Among the elderly (age 65+) is the suicide rate higher for men or women? _____

17. The low suicide rate observed in elderly Native Americans has been explained as being due to the _____ given to the aged in the Native American culture.

18. The first suicide prevention program in the United States was the _____.

19. A person without professional training who provides mental health services under the supervision of a mental health professional is typically called a

    _____.

20.   Workers at a suicide prevention center attempt to assess the caller's potential for suicide by using a _____ scale.

EXPLANATIONS OF DIFFICULT MATERIAL

A major problem for suicide research is that the subjects are no longer alive. The methods used to explore questions about suicide are retrospective analysis (also called the psychological autopsy) and the study of people who have survived suicide attempts.

Retrospective analysis requires the research group to obtain information from relatives and friends concerning the person who committed suicide. There are potential problems with this method and with the data obtained. Relatives may not be objective in reporting information about the person who committed suicide; they may not recall relevant information; or they may be reluctant to cooperate with the research team. Also, some persons who have committed suicide may have been relatively isolated from their relatives and had few friends. Obviously the completeness and the quality of the information obtained may vary widely. Nevertheless, fairly complete data may be obtained on a considerable number of subjects.

A study of people who have survived suicide attempts has a different set of weaknesses. This method, in effect, assumes that the sample of suicide attempters who have survived is equivalent to a sample of persons who have committed suicide. This may not be the case. It seems obvious that attempters who have used relatively nonlethal methods, such as minor wrist-slashing or minimal drug ingestion, differ from people who have actually committed suicide. If the sample of attempters who survived were restricted to those who attempted suicide by a very lethal method, the assumption that this sample might be equivalent to people who had killed themselves would be more tenable. Obviously, careful sample selection can strengthen this research method and thus the validity of the findings obtained from the research.

ADDITIONAL READINGS

Cole, D. A. (1988). Hopelessness, social desirability, depression, and parasuicide in two college samples. *Journal of Consulting and Clinical Psychology, 56,* 131–136.

Curran, D. K. (1987). *Adolescent suicide behavior.* Washington, D.C.: Hemisphere.

Holden, C. (1986). Youth suicide: New research focuses on a growing social problem. *Science, 233,* 839–841.

Ivanoff, A., & Jang, S. J. (1991). The role of hopelessness and social desirability in predicting suicidal behavior: A study of prison inmates. *Journal of Consulting and Clinical Psychology, 59,* 394–399.

Roy, A. (Ed.) (1986). *Suicide.* Baltimore: Williams & Wilkins.

Roy, A., Segal, N. L., Centerwall, B. S., & Robinette, C. D. (1991). Suicide in twins. *Archives in General Psychiatry, 48,* 29–32.

Westerfeld, J. S., & Furr, S. R. (1987). Suicide and depression among college students. *Professional Psychology: Research and Practice, 18,* 119–123.

ANSWER KEY

Multiple-Choice Questions:

1d, 2c, 3a, 4b, 5a, 6b, 7a, 8b, 9c, 10a.

Short-Answer Questions:

1. parasuicides
2. intentioned
3. subintentioned death
4. retrospective analysis (or psychological autopsy)
5. divorced
6. whites
7. hopelessness
8. mood disorders, substance use disorders, schizophrenia
9. modeling (or contagion) effect
10. Thanatos
11. serotonin
12. egoistic, altruistic, anomic
13. sociocultural
14. teenagers
15. higher
16. men
17. respect
18. Los Angeles Suicide Prevention Center
19. paraprofessional
20. lethality

CHAPTER 11

PSYCHOLOGICAL FACTORS AND PHYSICAL DISORDERS

CHAPTER OVERVIEW

For centuries medical theory embraced the idea of *mind-body dualism*, but medical practitioners now recognize that many physical illnesses are *psychogenic,* or caused by psychological factors.

A person with a *factitious disorder with physical symptoms* intentionally produces or feigns symptoms to meet a psychological need. Unlike the malingerer, this person receives no external advantage by producing symptoms. Some people feign symptoms of a mental disorder; this condition is diagnosed as *factitious disorder with psychological symptoms.* Factitious disorders are poorly understood and effective treatments have not been developed.

People with *somatoform disorders*—what Freud called *neuroses*—do not consciously will their symptoms or exercise any control over them, but again no organic cause can be found. *Hysterical disorders* involve a loss or alteration of physical functioning. People whose psychological problems are converted into physical symptoms are said to have *conversion disorders*. People with *somatization disorders* (also known as *Briquet's syndrome*) have 13 or more physical ailments with no organic basis over many years. *Somatoform pain disorder* is characterized by severe and prolonged pain

97

with no known physical cause. These hysterical disorders are usually accompanied by a nonchalant attitude known as *la belle indifférence*, neurological and anatomical inconsistencies, an unexpected course of development, and physical abilities inconsistent with the symptoms. People with *preoccupation somatoform disorders* believe that minimal physical symptoms indicate a serious problem. *Hypochondriasis* is similar to a somatization disorder but is distinguished by an anxiety level that is more significant than the physical symptoms. *Body dysmorphic disorders (dysmorphobias)* are characterized by preoccupation with some imagined or minimal physical defect.

Freud traced the hysterical disorders to an unresolved *Electra complex*. Today most psychodynamic theorists believe that they are caused by some conflict that arouses anxiety, which is then converted into physical symptoms. These symptoms bring a *primary gain* (they disguise the internal conflict) and a *secondary gain* (they enable one to avoid unpleasant activities or to win sympathy). Cognitive theorists view the hysterical disorders as forms of communication. Behavioral theorists believe they bring the sufferer rewards. Most treatments for the hysterical disorders focus on insight, suggestion, or confrontation. Diagnosis is difficult, and some physical disorders are misdiagnosed as somatoform disorders.

Psychophysiological disorders are thought to result from an interaction of psychological and physical factors. They include *ulcers, asthma, chronic headaches, hypertension,* and *coronary heart disease.* The *disregulation model* proposes that these disorders result from disruption of *negative feedback loops* between the brain and the rest of the body.

Among the factors that produce the physiological disorders are *cataclysmic stressors; personal stressors; background stressors;* idiosyncratic psychological reactions, such as *Type A personality;* and physiological dysfunctioning. Ordinarily, the *sympathetic nervous system* and the *parasympathetic nervous system*, subsystems of the *autonomic nervous system (ANS),* work together to produce *homeostasis* (stability), but they may fail to do so under stress. Hans Selye proposed that the typical response to stress is a *general adaptation syndrome,* consisting of three stages: *alarm, resistance,* and *exhaustion. Local somatic weaknesses, individual response specificity* and *autonomic learning* may also contribute to psychophysiological disorders. *Retrospective studies* and *prospective studies* have shown that stress contributes not only to psychophysiological disorders but also to *sudden death.*

Research in *psychoneuroimmunology*, a relatively new area of study, has shown that stress can interfere with the body's immune system by suppressing the action of *lymphocytes*, so that they fail to produce enough *antibodies* to destroy invading *antigens. Perceptions of control and the inhibited power motive style* of personality have also been shown to affect the functioning of the immune system.

The field of *behavioral medicine* combines physical and psychological interventions—*relaxation training, biofeedback training, meditation, hypnosis, self-instruction training (stress inoculation),* and *insight psychotherapy,* alone or in combination—to treat the psychophysiological disorders.

KEY TERMS

mind-body dualism

psychogenic

factitious disorders with physical symptoms

factitious disorders with psychological symptoms

somatoform disorders

hysterical disorders

conversion disorders

somatization disorders (Briquet's syndrome)

somatoform pain disorders

la belle indifférence

preoccupation somatoform disorders

hypochondriasis

body dysmorphic disorders (dysmorphobia)

Electra complex

primary gain

secondary gain

ulcers

asthma

chronic headaches

hypertension

coronary heart disease

disregulation model

negative feedback loops

cataclysmic stressors

personal stressors

background stressors

Type A personality

sympathetic nervous system

parasympathetic nervous system

autonomic nervous system (ANS)

homeostasis

general adaptation syndrome

local somatic weaknesses

individual response specificity

autonomic learning

retrospective studies

prospective studies

sudden death

psychoneuroimmunology

lymphocytes

antibodies

antigens

inhibited power motive style

behavioral medicine

relaxation training

biofeedback training

meditation

hypnosis

self-instruction training (stress inoculation)

insight psychotherapy

SAMPLE MULTIPLE-CHOICE QUESTIONS

1. A conversion disorder must be differentiated from:
    a. malingering
    b. an organic disorder
    c. both a and b
    d. neither a nor b

2. Which of the somatoform disorders is most likely to involve multiple physical symptoms and complaints?
    a. conversion disorder
    b. somatization disorder
    c. somatoform pain disorder
    d. body dysmorphic disorder

3. The symptom referred to as *la belle indifférence* is most commonly associated with:
    a. somatoform pain disorder
    b. hypochondriasis
    c. body dysmorphic disorder
    d. conversion disorder

4. Body dysmorphic disorder resembles:
    a. schizophrenia
    b. personality disorder
    c. phobic disorder
    d. panic disorder

5. Patients with conversion disorders respond best to which of the following approaches or interventions?
    a. confrontational approach
    b. insight approach
    c. exposure approach
    d. response-prevention intervention

6. Ulcers, asthma, and hypertension are classified as:
    a. psychophysiological disorders
    b. somatization disorders
    c. conversion disorders
    d. none of the above

7. The concept of negative feedback loops figures prominently in which explanation of the traditional psychophysiological disorders?
a. psychodynamic view
b. disregulation model
c. cognitive model
d. behavioral view

8. Which branch of the autonomic nervous system is involved in emotional arousal?
a. sympathetic nervous system
b. parasympathetic nervous system
c. peripheral nervous system
d. none of the above

9. The third stage in Hans Selye's general adaptation syndrome is the:
a. resistance stage
b. exhaustion stage
c. recovery stage
d. feedback stage

10. The link between stress and deficient functioning of the immune system has been supported by:
a. animal studies
b. human studies
c. both a and b
d. neither a nor b

SAMPLE SHORT-ANSWER QUESTIONS

1. People who intentionally produce psychological or physical symptoms to meet internal psychological needs are said to have a(n) _____ disorder.

2. Munchausen syndrome is a form of _____ disorder.

3. List the three somatoform disorders referred to as hysterical disorders.

_____
_____
_____

4. List the two somatoform disorders referred to as preoccupation disorders.

   _____

   _____

5. Somatization disorder is also known as

   _____ .

6. People who receive a diagnosis of hypochondriasis tend to interpret relatively minor physical discomforts as signs of a serious _____ .

7. The preoccupation somatoform disorders are usually explained the same way as the _____ .

8. Freud viewed conversion disorders as stemming from conflicts developed during the _____ stage of psychosexual development.

9. Hysterical symptoms that enable a person to avoid unpleasant activities or gain sympathy are said to bring _____ gain.

10. Cognitive theorists view hysterical disorders as a form of

    _____ .

11. Behavioral theorists believe that the somatoform disorders bring the patients _____ .

12. Chronic high blood pressure caused by a combination of psychological and physiological factors is called

    _____ .

13. Type A personality is a personality style that is associated with which physical disorder?

    _____

14. Which branch of the autonomic nervous system becomes activated after a danger has passed?

    _____

15. Recent research suggests that stress may contribute to viral and bacterial infections by virtue of its effect on the body's _____ .

16. The Holmes and Rahe Social Adjustment Rating Scale is intended to measure the amount of _____ in a person's life.

17. Which of the two types of studies that have used the Holmes and Rahe scale is considered to be methodologically stronger? _____

18. Research on life changes suggests that _____ change is more closely linked to the onset of illness.

19. The field of treatment that combines psychological and physical interventions to treat or prevent medical problems is known as

_____.

20. The term "stress inoculation" has been applied to _____ interventions.

EXPLANATIONS OF DIFFICULT MATERIAL

The somatoform disorders are difficult to diagnose. Their symptoms (especially those of the conversion disorders, somatization disorders, and hypochondriasis) can overlap to a considerable extent with those of factitious disorders, psychophysiological disorders, malingering, and undiagnosed physical illnesses. The critical differences among these disorders can be specified, but the differentiation is sometimes difficult to accomplish in practice. The symptoms of the somatoform, psychophysiological, and physical disorders are involuntary, but those of the factitious disorders and malingering are under voluntary control.

The differentiation of factitious disorders from malingering is based on the fact that the malingerer has an obvious external goal—insurance benefits, say—that the symptoms are designed to achieve, whereas the person with a factitious disorder has no external goal other than the attentions of health providers. The symptoms of the somatoform disorders are linked to psychological factors. Consequently, a careful review of the person's recent and current life situation may reveal evidence of conflicts or stresses that could cause physical symptoms for which no organic cause is found.

The symptoms of a psychophysiological disorder are produced by a physical mechanism, yet they can be exacerbated by psychological factors, and in this sense these disorders can be said to resemble the somatoform disorders. Finally, there is the possibility that physical disorders can be misdiagnosed as somatoform disorders. Some medical problems present vague and confusing symptoms and are difficult to diagnose.

The reliability of the classifications of mental disorders is less than perfect, and it seems likely that current medical diagnosis is not always reliable either. Research makes it clear that physical disorders are indeed sometimes misdiagnosed as somatoform disorders.

ADDITIONAL READINGS

Denney, R. R., Stephenson, L. A., Penick, E., & Weller, R. (1988). Lymphocyte subclasses and depression. *Journal of Abnormal Psychology, 97,* 499–502.

Gatchel, R. J., & Baum, A. (1988). *An introduction to health psychology.* New York: Random House.

Golding, J. M., Smith, G. R., Jr., & Kashner, T. M. (1991). Does somatization disorder occur in men?: Clinical characteristics of women and men with multiple unexplained somatic symptoms. *Archives of General Psychiatry, 48,* 231–235.

Keefe, F. J., & Williams, D. A. (1989). New directions in pain assessment and treatment. *Clinical Psychology Review, 9,* 549–568.

Rodin, J., & Salovey, P. (1989). Health psychology. *Annual Review of Psychology, 40,* 533–580.

Sarafino, E. P. (1990). *Health psychology: Biopsychosocial interactions.* New York: Wiley.

Taylor, G. R., Neale, L. S., & Dardano, J. R. (1986). Immunological analyses of U.S. space shuttle crew members. *Aviation, Space, and Environmental Medicine, 57,* 213–217.

ANSWER KEY

Multiple-Choice Questions:

1c, 2b, 3d, 4c, 5b, 6a, 7b, 8a, 9b, 10c.

Short-Answer Questions:

1. factitious disorder
2. factitious disorder
3. conversion disorders, somatization disorders, somatoform pain disorders
4. hypochondriasis, body dysmorphic disorder
5. Briquet's syndrome
6. physical illness or disease

7. phobias (or simple phobias)
8. phallic
9. secondary
10. communication
11. reinforcement (or reward)
12. essential hypertension
13. coronary heart disease
14. parasympathetic nervous system
15. immune system
16. stress
17. prospective studies
18. uncontrollable
19. behavioral medicine
20. cognitive

CHAPTER 12

EATING DISORDERS

CHAPTER OVERVIEW

The two major eating disorders, anorexia nervosa and bulimia nervosa, show a strong tendency to begin in adolescence, and girls and young women are greatly overrepresented among their victims.

Victims of *anorexia nervosa* experience such a pervasive fear of becoming fat that they diet to excess, lose a great amount of weight, and are subject to serious medical complications. The most common is *amenorrhea*. *Bulimia nervosa,* also known as the binge-purge syndrome, involves an excessive preoccupation with weight and body shape and a behavior pattern of recurrent binge eating followed by self-induced vomiting or other attempts to prevent weight gain. Bulimia nervosa is also associated with serious medical problems. Most persons with bulimia maintain their weight within the normal range, but a few become overweight and a few become dangerously underweight. Those who lose excessive weight are said to have *bulimic anorexia nervosa,* whereas persons who maintain a very low weight exclusively by dieting are said to have *restrictive anorexia nervosa.*

Theorists generally view eating disorders from a *multidimensional risk perspective,* which identifies factors that put a person at risk for an eating disorder. These factors include sociocultural pressures, such as the current emphasis on thinness in Western society; family environment, as in the enmeshed family pattern; ego deficiencies and cognitive disturbances, as a result of ineffective parents who fail to attend to a child's needs; biological factors; and mood disorders, primarily depression. Biological researchers have discovered that hunger is activated by the *lateral hypothalamus (LH)* and depressed by the *ventromedial hypothalamus (VMH)*. It is thought that the LH and VMH work together to predispose a person to maintain a particular weight, or *weight set point,* and to control the *metabolic rate.* When people's weight drops below their set point, the hypothalamus acts to produce *hyperlipogenesis,* or the retention of abnormal amounts of fat in the fat cells. Thus it becomes increasingly harder to lose weight by dieting. Some people manage to control their eating almost completely and become anorexic; others develop the binge-purge syndrome.

The various risk factors may be seen as *predispositions* (such as Western society's emphasis on thinness), *precipitants* (such as unflattering remarks about one's appearance), and *perpetuators* (such as the physical changes caused by dieting that maintain the pattern).

The first step in treatment for anorexia nervosa is to increase the patient's weight quickly. Supportive nursing care in conjunction with a high-calorie diet is the most favored method, but antipsychotic drugs, antidepressant medications, and operant conditioning techniques have had some successes also. Approaches used to address broader issues so that improvement may be more lasting have included individual, group, and especially family therapy. Treatment for bulimia is also aimed at eliminating the pathological eating pattern and at addressing issues that may cause the problem to recur. Exposure and response prevention techniques are often useful in breaking the pattern of binging and purging. Individual insight therapy, psychodynamic or cognitive, is a common form of treatment, and antidepressant medication is useful in the treatment of bulimia. Group therapy is incorporated into most treatment programs.

KEY TERMS

anorexia nervosa

bulimia nervosa

amenorrhea

bulimic anorexia nervosa

restrictive anorexia nervosa

multidimensional risk factors

lateral hypothalamus (LH)

ventromedial hypothalamus (VMH)

weight set point

metabolic rate

hyperlipogenesis

predispositions

precipitants

perpetuators

SAMPLE MULTIPLE-CHOICE QUESTIONS

1. Approximately what proportion of people with anorexia nervosa are girls and women?
   a. 95%
   b. 75%
   c. 60%
   d. 50%

2. When anorexic and control subjects looked at a
    photograph of themselves through a special lens that
    they could manipulate until the image shown was what
    they estimated their actual size to be, anorexics:
    a. underestimated their body size
    b. overestimated their body size
    c. performed the same as controls

3. The most common medical problem of a woman with
    anorexia is:
    a. congestive heart failure
    b. electrolyte imbalances
    c. metabolic imbalances
    d. amenorrhea

4. The weight of people with bulimia nervosa usually stays:
    a. below normal
    b. above normal
    c. within the normal range

5. During a binge, the person with bulimia nervosa usually
    feels:
    a. intensely angry
    b. very guilty
    c. unable to stop eating
    d. unaware of what is happening

6. Which of the following characteristics is or are common
    to anorexia and bulimia?
    a. a preoccupation with food
    b. fear of becoming obese
    c. both a and b
    d. neither a nor b

7. The study that analyzed heights, weights, and ages of
    contestants in the Miss America Pageant over a number
    of years supported which of the following as a factor in
    the development of eating disorders?
    a. family environment
    b. sociocultural pressures
    c. biological factors
    d. psychodynamic factors

8. Family systems theorists emphasize which of the
    following concepts in their study of the family?
    a. ego boundaries
    b. reinforcement
    c. homeostasis
    d. the sick individual

9. Minuchin believes that the family pattern that often
    leads to eating disorders is one in which:
    a. family members are overinvolved with one another
    b. family members are uncaring with respect to one
    another
    c. one family member is overly domineering
    d. family members are hostile and angry with one
    another

10. Research indicates a relationship between eating
    disorders and:
    a. anxiety disorders
    b. schizophrenia
    c. mood disorders
    d. none of the above

SAMPLE SHORT-ANSWER QUESTIONS

1. DSM-III-R specifies as a criterion for anorexia nervosa
    that the person be _____ percent below normal or
    expected body weight.

2. What three cognitive disturbances are found in patients
    with anorexia nervosa?

    _____

    _____

    _____

3. When subjects were put on a semistarvation diet for six
    months, thoughts of food became their

    _____.

4. The DSM-III-R definition of bulimia nervosa requires
    recurrent episodes of binge eating, averaging at least two
    episodes per _____.

5. DSM-III-R also specifies that for a diagnosis of bulimia
    nervosa, certain methods be used habitually to prevent
    weight gain. Four of these methods are

    _____

    _____

    _____

    _____

6. Is bulimia nervosa more common in females or in males? _____

7. The central feature of bulimia nervosa is _____.

8. Persons with which eating disorder(s) are preoccupied with their weight? _____

9. Persons with which eating disorder are more likely to be aware that they are engaging in a pathological pattern of behavior?

    _____

10. What sociocultural pressure has contributed to the development of eating disorders?

    _____

11. Members of which three occupational groups or subcultures should be more vulnerable than the general population to eating disorders?

    _____
    _____
    _____

12. Until recent years, were eating disorders more common in the higher or lower socioeconomic groups?

    _____

13. The descriptive term that Minuchin applies to the family pattern that often leads to eating disorders is

    _____

14. Hilde Bruch's theory of eating disorders incorporates ideas from which two perspectives?

    _____
    _____

15. The brain area that has been the focus of attention for researchers studying the development and maintenance of eating disorders is the _____.

16. The risk factors associated with the eating disorders are divided into what three categories?

    _____
    _____
    _____

17. What class of drugs has been the most helpful in altering dysfunctional eating patterns?

_____

18. A form of therapy applied to help people with anorexia nervosa change their misconceptions about eating and weight is _____.

19. The behavior therapy technique used to break the binge-purge cycle is _____.

20. A form of therapy that is incorporated into most treatment programs for people with bulimia is

_____.

EXPLANATIONS OF DIFFICULT MATERIAL

It is clear that even when eating disorders are viewed from the multidimensional risk perspective, the causes of anorexia nervosa and bulimia nervosa are not completely understood. The pressures to be thin are certainly pervasive in our society, yet most women who are exposed to these pressures do not develop anorexia nervosa. Perhaps the presence or absence of other risk factors determines whether a particular individual develops an eating disorder. The families of people with eating disorders have a history of emphasizing appearance, thinness, and dieting. Another risk factor is a poor sense of autonomy and control. Children of ineffective parents may fail to develop self-reliance, and consequently may feel pressures to establish autonomy but lack the personal resources to do so. Such children may find that their eating is the one area they can control. Feeling helpless in all other respects, such children may find their success in controlling their weight so reinforcing that they persist in losing weight until they endanger their health and even their lives.

Children of effective parents, however, do not feel helpless and so are less affected by the society's emphasis on thinness even if their families emphasize appearance and dieting. Thus a risk factor may lead to a disorder in a person who is exposed to a second risk factor but not in another person who is not exposed to the second risk factor. Obviously, the more risk factors that enter the picture, the more complicated it becomes.

ADDITIONAL READINGS

Heatherton, T. F., & Baumeister, R. F. (1991). Binge eating as escape from self-awareness. *Psychological Bulletin, 110,* 86–108.

Hinz, L. D., & Williamson, D. A. (1987). Bulimia and depression: A review of the affective variant hypothesis. *Psychological Bulletin, 102,* 105–158.

Hsu, L. K. G. (1989). The gender gap in eating disorders: Why are the eating disorders more common in women? *Clinical Psychology Review, 9,* 393–407.

Pike, K. M., & Rodin, J. (1991). Mothers, daughters, and disordered eating. *Journal of Abnormal Psychology, 100,* 198–204.

Strauss, J., & Ryan, R. M. (1987). Autonomy disturbances in subtypes of anorexia nervosa. *Journal of Abnormal Psychology, 96,* 254–258.

Strober, M., & Humphrey, L. L. (1987). Familial contributions to the etiology and course of anorexia nervosa and bulimia. *Journal of Consulting and Clinical Psychology, 55,* 654–659.

Williamson, D. A. (1990). *Assessment of eating disorders: Obesity, anorexia, and bulimia nervosa.* New York: Pergamon.

ANSWER KEY

Multiple-Choice Questions:

1a, 2b, 3d, 4c, 5c, 6c, 7b, 8c, 9a, 10c.

Short-Answer Questions:

1. 15
2. distorted body image, distorted internal perceptions, maladaptive thinking
3. preoccupation
4. week
5. self-induced vomiting, use of laxatives or diuretics, strict dieting or fasting, vigorous exercise
6. females
7. binge eating
8. anorexia nervosa and bulimia nervosa
9. bulimia nervosa
10. emphasis on thinness
11. dancers, models, actors
12. higher
13. enmeshed

14.   psychodynamic, cognitive
15.   hypothalamus
16.   predispositions, precipitants, perpetuators
17.   antidepressants
18.   cognitive therapy
19.   exposure and response prevention
20.   group therapy

CHAPTER 13

SUBSTANCE USE DISORDERS

CHAPTER OVERVIEW

Substance abuse may lead to a temporary *organic brain syndrome,* characterized by altered behavior, emotion, or thought. Excessive use of alcohol, for instance, leads to *intoxication* (poisoning); LSD causes *hallucinosis. Substance use disorder* is a longer-term pattern of maladaptive behavior that can take the form of *substance abuse* (such excessive reliance on a drug that it affects one's life) or *substance dependence* (development of *tolerance* to the drug and *withdrawal symptoms* if its use is discontinued).

The most common of the *depressants,* which slow the activity of the central nervous system, is alcohol. In 5 to 10 percent of people who are alcohol dependent, withdrawal symptoms take the form of *alcohol withdrawal delirium (delirium tremens,* or *the DT's),* typically characterized by terrifying visual hallucinations. *Alcoholic hallucinosis,* consisting of auditory hallucinations, is rarer. Chronic abuse of alcohol can cause fatal *cirrhosis,* or damage to the liver. Since alcohol is high in calories but has virtually no food value, chronic excessive alcohol drinking can lead to malnutrition and to *Wernicke's encephalopathy,* a potentially fatal neurological disease; untreated, it may develop into *Korsakoff's syndrome (alcohol amnestic disorder),* marked by such loss of memory that victims are given to *confabulating*—spontaneously making up things to fill in the gaps. The *sedative-hypnotic drugs* include

119

the benzodiazepines, or antianxiety drugs, and barbiturates. Both can lead to dependence. Withdrawal from the barbiturates may cause *barbiturate withdrawal delirium,* similar to delirium tremens, or *barbiturate amnestic disorder (Korsakoff's syndrome).*

Morphine is derived from opium; *heroin* is a form of morphine. These and other opioid drugs are known collectively as *narcotics.* Heroin brings on a brief *rush,* followed by several hours of relaxed euphoria known as a *high* or *nod.* After people become habituated to heroin, however, they need it simply to function normally. Addicts who inject the drug with unsterile needles are at risk for AIDS and other infections. *Quinine*, often added to heroin to counter infections, can itself cause death. *Stimulants* increase the activity of the central nervous system. *Cocaine*, the most powerful natural stimulant known, is processed into *hydrochloride powder.* Very high doses lead to *cocaine intoxication* and sometimes to *cocaine psychosis.* *Free-basing* is a technique of separating the pure cocaine alkoloid from processed cocaine; *crack* is a ready-to-smoke free-base cocaine. Cocaine's effects are powerful and dangerous. *Amphetamines* are also stimulants; their effects are similar to those of cocaine.

Hallucinogens, which cause changes in sensory perception, include the *psychedelic drugs* and cannabis. *LSD (lysergic acid diethylamide)* causes *hallucinogenic hallucinosis.* Hallucinations are primarily visual but may involve the other senses. In an effect called *synesthesia,* the senses may appear to cross, so that sounds are seen and colors are heard. These experiences may be terrifying. Some users develop a *hallucinogen delusional disorder* in which the hallucinations persist. Others develop a *hallucinogen mood disorder.* About 25 percent of users experience *flashbacks. Cannabis*, produced from hemp, comes in three forms: *hashish* (the most powerful), *ganja* (intermediate), and *marijuana* (weakest). *Cannabis intoxication* may lead to *cannabis delusional disorder,* in which users believe that other people are hostile to them.

Some drugs are so similar in their actions that users of one drug may develop a *cross-tolerance* to another. When two or more drugs are in the body at the same time, they may *potentiate* (enhance) each other's effects, producing a *synergistic effect.* The use of multiple drugs, or *polydrug use,* is a dangerous practice.

Twin studies suggest a genetic predisposition to substance abuse. Psychodynamic theorists believe that people whose

needs were not satisfied in childhood are particularly
vulnerable to drugs. Behaviorists stress the reinforcing effect of
the reduction of tension produced by drugs. Some behaviorists
explain the unpleasant effects of excessive and chronic use by
the *opponent-process theory*. Sociocultural theorists propose
that societal stress encourages drug abuse.

Behavioral treatments include *aversive conditioning, covert
sensitization, behavioral self-control training (BSCT),* and
relapse-prevention training. Biological techniques include
detoxification, the use of *antagonist drugs,* and *methadone
maintenance programs*. The best known self-help program is
Alcoholics Anonymous (AA). Synanon, a program for
narcotics abusers, took a confrontational approach.
Eventually it became one of the many *residential treatment
centers,* or *therapeutic communities,* that address the needs of
addicts.

KEY TERMS

organic mental syndrome

intoxication

hallucinosis

substance use disorders

substance abuse

substance dependence

tolerance

withdrawal symptoms

depressants

alcoholism

alcohol withdrawal delirium (delirium tremens, the DT's)

alcoholic hallucinosis

cirrhosis

Wernicke's encephalopathy

Korsakoff's syndrome (alcohol amnestic disorder)

confabulating

sedative-hypnotic drugs

barbiturate withdrawal delirium

barbiturate amnestic disorder

morphine

heroin

narcotics

rush

high (nod)

quinine

stimulants

cocaine

hydrochloride powder

cocaine intoxication

cocaine psychosis

free-basing

crack

hallucinogens

psychedelic drugs

LSD (lysergic acid diethylamide)

hallucinogenic hallucinosis

synesthesia

hallucinogen delusional disorder

hallucinogen mood disorder

flashbacks

cannabis

hashish

ganja

marijuana

cannabis intoxication

cannabis delusional disorder

cross-tolerance

potentiate

synergistic effect

polydrug use

opponent-process theory

aversive conditioning

covert sensitization

behavioral self-control training (BSCT)

relapse-prevention training

detoxification

antagonist drugs

Alcoholics Anonymous

Synanon

residential treatment center (therapeutic community)

SAMPLE
MULTIPLE-CHOICE
QUESTIONS

1. The development of tolerance and the experience of withdrawal symptoms occur in:
   a. substance abuse
   b. substance dependence
   c. both a and b
   d. neither a nor b

2. Alcohol is a:
   a. stimulant
   b. hallucinogen
   c. depressant
   d. combination drug

3. The barbiturates are classified as:
   a. stimulants
   b. hallucinogens
   c. depressants
   d. combination drugs

4. Which of the following drugs is derived from opium?
   a. methadone
   b. hashish
   c. quinine
   d. morphine

5. Which of the following is classified as a stimulant?
   a. cocaine
   b. cannabis
   c. opioids
   d. alcohol

6. LSD is classified as a(n):
   a. stimulant
   b. depressant
   c. hallucinogen
   d. analgesic

7. Tetrahydrocannabinol(THC) is the active ingredient in:
   a. marijuana
   b. LSD
   c. cocaine
   d. opioids

8. Goodwin reported that the highest rate of alcoholism was found in adoptees who had:
   a. alcoholic adoptive parents
   b. nonalcoholic adoptive parents
   c. alcoholic biological parents
   d. nonalcoholic biological parents

9. A behavioral technique often used to treat substance use disorders is:
   a. modeling
   b. systematic desensitization
   c. aversive conditioning
   d. client-centered therapy

10. Disulfiram (Antabuse) is an antagonist drug for:
    a. narcotic drugs
    b. alcohol
    c. amphetamines
    d. antianxiety drugs

SAMPLE
SHORT-ANSWER
QUESTIONS

1. What are the two categories of substance use disorders?
    _____
    _____

2. A person who uses a drug to excess and then suddenly stops taking the drug experiences_____.

3. Drugs that slow the activity of the central nervous system are called
    _____.

4. List three groups of depressants.
    _____
    _____
    _____

5. When people whose memory is severely impaired by alcohol abuse make up things to fill in what they cannot remember, they are said to be
    _____.

6. The antianxiety drugs belong to which group of drugs?
    _____

7. It has been found that brain receptor sites that ordinarily receive endorphins will react in the same way if they instead receive _____.

8. The two best-known stimulant drugs are
    _____
    and _____.

9. Stimulants are drugs that increase the activity of the _____ nervous system.

10. Two common and casual uses of amphetamines are _____and _____.

11. The experience of crossed senses, such as hearing a color, under the influence of LSD is referred to as
    _____.

12. The most powerful form of cannabis is
    _____.

13. Some drugs are so similar in their action that as people build up a tolerance for one drug, they are also developing a tolerance for the others. This effect is called _____.

14. Alcohol taken by a person who has also taken antianxiety drugs produces a

    _____.

15. A twin study investigating alcohol abuse found that the identical twins had a higher _____ rate.

16. Which explanation of substance use disorders emphasizes a "substance abuse personality"?

    _____

17. The behavioral view of substance abuse emphasizes which effects of a drug?

    _____

18. The aversive conditioning technique that requires alcoholics to imagine unpleasant scenes is called

    _____.

19. Systematic and medically supervised withdrawal from a drug is called _____.

20. In methadone maintenance programs, methadone is given as a substitute for _____.

EXPLANATIONS OF DIFFICULT MATERIAL

Research makes it clear that children whose parents are alcoholics are more likely than other children to become alcoholics. Moreover, the same effect is found among such children who were raised by nonalcoholic adoptive parents. Hence, a predisposition to develop alcoholism may be inherited. Yet even if biological factors do predispose some people to develop alcoholism, only some of those people eventually become alcoholics. Why?

One possibile answer relates to additional contributing factors. The term "predisposition" seems to imply a necessity for additional factors in the causal path to the development of alcoholism. One such factor may be the one emphasized by the behaviorists: the reduction of tension brought about by alcohol. If the drinking of alcohol reduces a person's tension, and the reduction of tension reinforces the use of alcohol, the person is likely to drink alcohol again if stresses mount. People who have learned more effective methods of coping with stress will be less likely to turn to alcohol under stress. When these people do drink, they are less likely to experience a reduction of stress (reinforcement) as a result. Consequently, when they experience stress again later, they will not be so likely to drink alcohol. Thus, those people who have an inherited predisposition to alcohol abuse but also have effective coping skills may drink alcohol not at all or only socially and never become alcoholic. People who have the inherited predisposition but lack effective skills for coping with stress may be likely to develop alcoholism. This explanation is only a hypothesis; the causal factors that lead to alcoholism have not yet been identified with certainty.

ADDITIONAL READINGS

Blane, H. T., & Leonard, K. E. (Eds.) (1987). *Psychological theories of drinking and alcoholism.* New York: Guilford.

Bushman, B. J., & Cooper, H. M. (1990). Effect of alcohol on human aggression: An integrative research review. *Psychological Bulletin, 107,* 341–354.

Chiauzzi, E. J. (1991). *Preventing relapses in the addictions.* New York: Pergamon.

Christiansen, B. C., Smith, G. T., Roehling, P. V., & Goldman, M. S. (1989). Using alcohol expectancies to predict adolescent drinking behavior after one year. *Journal of Consulting and Clinical Psychology, 57,* 93–99.

Finney, J. W., & Moos, R. H. (1991). The long-term course of treated alcoholism: I. Mortality, relapse, and remission rates and comparisons with community controls. *Journal of Studies on Alcohol, 52,* 44–54.

Hall, S. M., Havassy, B. F., & Wasserman, D. A. (1990). Commitment to abstinence and acute stress in relapse to alcohol, opiates, and nicotine. *Journal of Consulting and Clinical Psychology, 58,*175–181.

Julian, R. M. (1991). *A primer of drug action* (6th ed.). New York: W. H. Freeman.

McKim, W. A. (1990). *Drugs and behavior: An introduction to behavioral pharmacology* (2nd ed.). Englewood Cliffs, N.J.: Prentice-Hall.

Schuckit, M. A. (1989). *Drug and alcohol abuse: A clinical guide to diagnosis and treatment* (3rd ed.). New York: Plenum.

Segal, B. (1988). *Drugs and behavior.* New York: Gardner.

Windle, M., & Searles, J. S. (Eds.) (1990). *Children of alcoholics: Critical perspectives.* New York: Guilford.

ANSWER KEY

Multiple-Choice Questions:

1b, 2c, 3c, 4d, 5a, 6c, 7a, 8c, 9c, 10b.

Short-Answer Questions:

1. substance abuse, substance dependence
2. withdrawal (or withdrawal symptoms)
3. depressants
4. alcohol, sedative-hypnotic drugs, opioids
5. confabulating
6. sedative-hypnotic
7. heroin (or another opioid)
8. cocaine, amphetamines
9. central
10. to stay awake, to reduce appetite and weight
11. synesthesia
12. hashish
13. cross-tolerance
14. synergistic effect
15. concordance
16. psychodynamic
17. reinforcement
18. covert sensitization
19. detoxification
20. heroin

CHAPTER 14

SEXUAL DISORDERS

CHAPTER OVERVIEW

There are two types of sexual disorders. *Sexual dysfunctions* are impairments of some aspect of the sexual response cycle. *Paraphilias* are recurrent sexual urges in response to objects or situations that the larger society regards as inappropriate.

The sexual dysfunctions are classified according to the phase (desire, arousal, orgasm, resolution) of the sexual response cycle that is affected. *Hypoactive sexual desire* (lack of interest in sex) and *sexual aversion* are disorders of the desire phase. *Sexual arousal disorders* are characterized by a failure of either physical responses (lubrication or genital swelling in women, penile erection in men) or subjective excitement and pleasure, or both.

The most common male dysfunction of the orgasm phase is *premature ejaculation; inhibited male orgasm* despite adequate stimulation is much rarer. *Inhibited female orgasm* during intercourse is generally not considered a dysfunction if the woman can achieve orgasm by direct stimulation of the clitoris. *Vaginismus* (spastic contractions of the vaginal muscles that prevent the penis from entering) and *dyspareunia* ("painful mating") are not related to any specific phase of the sexual response cycle. A low level of the male hormone *testosterone* or of *luteinizing hormone,* which stimulates testosterone production, may lower the sex drive in both men and women.

Women's sex drive is also influenced by an abnormally low or high level of the female hormone *estrogen*. A high level of the hormone *prolactin* also interferes with the sex drive of both sexes, as do many drugs, physical illnesses, and psychological factors. A major psychological factor in failure of erection is *performance anxiety* and *the spectator role*.

Psychodynamic theorists considered the sexual dysfunctions untreatable. Behavioral therapists had limited success with systematic desensitization. Masters and Johnson revolutionized the treatment of these disorders with their "sex therapy," which has cognitive, behavioral, and communication components.

The paraphilias are sexual behavior patterns in which an unusual inanimate object, the infliction of suffering or pain, or a nonconsenting partner becomes the exclusive or preferred mode of sexual arousal. *Fetishism* is the displacement of sexual desire to an object or body part. *Transvestic fetishism* (or *transvestism* or *cross-dressing*) is the need to dress in clothes of the opposite sex to become sexually aroused. The preferred sex partners of people subject to *pedophilia* are children. *Exhibitionism* is the acting out of sexual fantasies by exposing one's genitals to another person in the hope of eliciting a reaction of shock. *Voyeurism* is a disorder in which a person seeks sexual arousal by secretly watching people as they undress or engage in intercourse. A person subject to *frotteurism* seeks sexual pleasure by rubbing his genitals against a woman or fondling her in a crowded public place. *Sexual masochism* is a pattern of seeking sexual pleasure through suffering. *Sexual sadism* is a pattern of seeking sexual pleasure through the infliction of physical or psychological pain on others.

Nearly all people who receive a diagnosis of paraphilia are men. The causes of these disorders are uncertain but immaturity is thought to play a large part in them. Behaviorists attribute fetishism, masochism, and sadism to classical conditioning and transvestism to operant conditioning; they consider voyeurism to be a learned behavior, and propose that modeling may also play a role in sadism. Aversion therapy and covert sensitization are the usual treatments.

KEY TERMS

sexual dysfunctions

paraphilias

hypoactive sexual desire

sexual aversion

sexual arousal disorders

premature ejaculation

inhibited male orgasm

inhibited female orgasm

vaginismus

voyeurism

dyspareunia

testosterone

luteinizing hormone

estrogen

prolactin

performance anxiety and the spectator role

fetishism

transvestic fetishism (transvestism, cross-dressing)

pedophilia

exhibitionism

frotteurism

sexual masochism

sexual sadism

SAMPLE
MULTIPLE-CHOICE
QUESTIONS

1. With which phase of the sexual response cycle is no
    sexual dysfunction associated?
    a. desire phase
    b. arousal phase
    c. orgasm phase
    d. resolution phase

2. Premature ejaculation is a sexual dysfunction involving
    which phase of the sexual response cycle?
    a. desire phase
    b. arousal phase
    c. orgasm phase
    d. resolution phase

3. Testosterone is an important factor in the sex drive of:
    a. men
    b. women
    c. both a and b
    d. neither a nor b

4. Which of the following drugs reduces the sex drive?
    a. antianxiety drugs
    b. antipsychotic drugs
    c. both a and b
    d. neither a nor b

5. The majority of cases of erectile dysfunction are:
    a. entirely psychological
    b. entirely organic
    c. partially organic and partially psychological

6. Nocturnal penile tumescence is used as a means of
    evaluating:
    a. premature ejaculation
    b. inhibited ejaculation
    c. erectile failure
    d. dyspareunia

7. When men subject to erectile failure and normally functioning men subjectively rated the degree of their erections in response to an erotic film, a gauge attached to each man's penis indicated that:
a. normal men perceived their erections accurately and dysfunctional men underestimated them
b. normal men overestimated their erections and dysfunctional men perceived them accurately
c. both groups overestimated
d. both groups underestimated

8. The "squeeze" procedure is used in the treatment of:
a. erectile failure
b. premature ejaculation
c. inhibited ejaculation
d. hypoactive sexual desire

9. Behaviorists propose that fetishes are acquired through:
a. modeling
b. classical conditioning
c. operant conditioning
d. latent learning

10. The paraphilia in which the person has recurrent sexual urges to touch or rub against a nonconsenting person is called:
a. voyeurism
b. frotteurism
c. partialism
d. pedophilia

SAMPLE SHORT-ANSWER QUESTIONS

1. The two categories of sexual disorders are
_____ and _____.

2. What are the four phases of the sexual response cycle?
_____
_____
_____
_____

3. What two sexual dysfunctions are associated with the desire phase of the sexual response cycle?
_____
_____

4. A sexual dysfunction experienced by a male during the arousal phase is _____.

5. Is dyspareunia more common in men or women? _____

6. In the past several years there has been a large increase in the number of men seeking therapy for which sexual dysfunction? _____

7. The primary female sex hormone is _____.

8. The primary male sex hormone is _____.

9. The major psychological mechanisms emphasized by Masters and Johnson as causing erectile failure are _____.

10. Psychological causes of inhibited ejaculation are thought to be similar to those of _____.

11. Research comparing sexually dysfunctional women with orgasmic women has shown that the use of sexual fantasies during sex with the current partner was more common in _____ women.

12. The text indicates that there is no physiological cause for _____.

13. Dyspareunia usually has a(n) _____ cause.

14. Behavioral theorists consider sexual dysfunctions to result from _____.

15. In discussing causal factors with a couple, sex therapists stress the principle of _____ responsibility.

16. The administration of an electric shock to a fetishist while he is imagining the sexually arousing object would be an example of _____ therapy.

17. The recurrent wish or need to dress in clothes of the opposite sex for the purpose of sexual arousal is called _____.

18. The sexual objects of people subject to pedophilia are
_____.

19. The paraphilia in which people have recurrent sexual urges to be humiliated, beaten, or made to suffer is called _____.

20. The paraphilia in which people have recurrent sexual urges to inflict pain and suffering on another person as a means of achieving sexual arousal is called

_____.

EXPLANATIONS OF DIFFICULT MATERIAL

Behavioral theorists consider classical conditioning to be the mechanism by which the fetishist acquires his fetish. If early sexual arousal is associated accidentally with the presence of a particular object, presumably the person will later become sexually aroused by that object. The one troublesome element of this explanation is its failure to account for the persistence of the fetish. In classical conditioning, the conditioned stimulus usually extinguishes if it occurs a few times without the original unconditioned stimulus (the stimulus that produced the original sexual excitement). If the fetishist were later to masturbate while fantasizing about the object, this activity could be said to represent additional conditioning trials. Consequently, the association between the object and the response of sexual excitement becomes greatly strengthened. Moreover, men for whom more normal sexual outlets are unsatisfying, limited, or nonexistent are the ones who are most likely to fantasize about an object that once was associated with sexual arousal. Men who have other satisfying sexual outlets are less likely to engage in such fantasies after an accidental pairing of an object and sexual arousal. For these men, any tendency to become sexually aroused by the conditioned stimulus is likely to extinguish rapidly.

ADDITIONAL READINGS

Alter-Reid, K., Gibbs, M. S., Lachenmeyer, J. R., Sigal, J., & Mossoth, N. A. (1986). Sexual abuse of children: A review of the empirical findings. *Clinical Psychology Review, 6,* 249–266.
Crooks, R., & Baur, K. (1990). *Our sexuality* (4th ed.). Menlo Park, Calif.: Benjamin/Cummings.
Forgac, G. E., & Michaels, E. J. (1982). Personality

characteristics of two types of male exhibitionists. *Journal of Abnormal Psychology, 91,* 287–293.

Hyde, J. S. (1990). *Understanding human sexuality* (4th ed.). New York: McGraw-Hill.

Leiblum, S. R., & Rosen, R. C. (Eds.) (1988). *Sexual desire disorders.* New York: Guilford.

Maletsky, B. M. (1980). Self-referred vs. court-referred sexually deviant patients: Success with assisted covert sensitization. *Behavior Therapy, 11,* 306–314.

Marshall, W. L., Jones, R., Ward, T., Johnston, P., & Barbaree, H. E. (1991). Treatment outcome with sex offenders. *Clinical Psychology Review, 11,* 465–485.

Overholser, J. C., & Beck, S. (1986). Multimethod assessment of rapists, child molesters, and three control groups on behavioral and psychological measures. *Journal of Consulting and Clinical Psychology, 54,* 682–687.

Storms, M. D. (1981). A theory of erotic orientation development. *Psychological Review, 88,* 340–353.

ANSWER KEY

Multiple-Choice Questions:

1d, 2c, 3c, 4d, 5c, 6c, 7a, 8b, 9b, 10b.

Short-Answer Questions:

1. sexual dysfunctions, paraphilias
2. desire, arousal, orgasm, resolution
3. hypoactive sexual desire, sexual aversion
4. male erectile disorder
5. women
6. hypoactive sexual desire
7. estrogen
8. testosterone
9. performance anxiety and the spectator role
10. erectile failure
11. orgasmic
12. vaginismus
13. physical
14. anxiety
15. mutual
16. aversion
17. transvestism (or transvestic fetishism or cross-dressing)
18. children
19. sexual masochism
20. sexual sadism

CHAPTER 15

SCHIZOPHRENIA

CHAPTER OVERVIEW

Schizophrenia is a *psychosis*, a condition in which individuals lose contact with reality to varying degrees. People who are diagnosed as schizophrenic may show considerable variation in their symptoms, and no single symptom is present in every case. Many schizophrenic people have *delusions*, ideas that have no basis in reality. People who have *delusions of persecution* believe they are being victimized. People with *delusions of reference* believe that words, objects, and events that have nothing to do with them have personal significance for them. People with *delusions of grandeur* believe that they are great historical figures or have special powers. *Delusions of control* are beliefs that other people are controlling one's actions, thoughts, and feelings, sometimes by *thought withdrawal, thought broadcasting,* or *thought insertion.* Somewhat less common are *somatic* and *religious delusions.*

Many people with schizophrenia display *formal thought disorders,* in particular *loose associations, word salad, neologisms, perseveration, clang,* and *blocking. High-risk studies* indicate that children of schizophrenic parents who themselves later develop schizophrenia display more formal thought disorders in adolescence than controls do. Schizophrenic people's disturbances in perception may include heightened sensitivity to sounds and sights or *sensory blunting* or *hallucinations,* not only auditory and visual but also tactile, somatic, and gustatory. Emotional disturbances may take the form of *blunted affect, flat affect,* or *inappropriate affect.* Many schizophrenic people are confused about their identity and even doubt their existence. They withdraw from other people and feel unable to make even simple decisions. Psychomotor disturbances—odd grimaces and gestures, a stilted gait—sometimes take extreme forms of *catatonia: catatonic stupor, catatonic rigidity, catatonic posturing, catatonic excitement,* and *waxy flexibility.*

The course of schizophrenia varies, but many patients progress from a *prodromal phase,* in which symptoms are not yet prominent but deterioration has begun, through an *active phase,* when symptoms are florid, to a *residual phase,* in which symptoms subside but the patient is still unable to function normally. The active phase may recur.

DSM-III-R distinguishes *disorganized schizophrenia,* characterized by confusion and incoherence; *catatonic schizophrenia,* in which psychomotor disturbances predominate; *paranoid schizophrenia,* an organized system of delusions; *undifferentiated type,* for patients who do not clearly fit one category; and *residual type,* for patients whose symptoms are no longer florid but have not disappeared. Clinicians also distinguish between *Type I schizophrenia,* characterized by *positive symptoms* of pathological excesses such as delusions and hallucinations, and *Type II schizophrenia,* characterized by *negative symptoms* of pathological deficits, such as flat affect and loss of volition.

Sociological theorists believe that "schizophrenia" is a label assigned to people who deviate from behavioral norms, which then becomes a self-fulfilling prophecy; yet the symptoms of the disorder are remarkably similar across cultures. Genetic researchers' belief that some people inherit a predisposition to schizophrenia is supported by studies of relatives of schizophrenic people, twin and adoption studies, and chromosomal mapping. The *dopamine hypothesis* posits a link between schizophrenia and the neurons that use the neurotransmitter dopamine. This link was suggested by the discovery that antipsychotic drugs alleviate *amphetamine psychosis,* which is traced to the action of amphetamines on the central nervous system. Researchers have discovered that antipsychotic drugs are *dopamine antagonists.* These discoveries appear to apply only to Type I schizophrenia; Type II schizophrenia has been linked to enlarged ventricles in the brain.

Psychodynamic theorists attribute schizophrenia to regression and restitutive efforts. Silvano Arieti believes that these patients regress to a level of primitive or *paleologic thought.* Behavioral theorists attribute the disorder to operant conditioning. Since theorists of both schools emphasize environmental factors, attention has been drawn to the families of schizophrenic people, particularly to the *schizophrenogenic mother.* Studies have not borne out this hypothesis. A related theory is the *double-bind hypothesis,* which research similarly fails to support. Family theorists propose that *marital schism* and *marital skew* push children into schizophrenic patterns. Many clinicians continue to suspect that family interactions may contribute to the onset of schizophrenia, if not to its origins. The most controversial view is that of the existentialist R. D. Laing, who sees schizophrenia as a constructive effort to free oneself from the confusion and misery caused by society and the family. Cognitive theorists propose that biological problems are exacerbated into delusions by cognitive processes when patients attempt to understand their experiences.

KEY TERMS

psychosis

schizophrenia

delusions

formal thought disorders

loose associations

word salad

neologisms

perseveration

clang

blocking

high-risk studies

sensory blunting

hallucinations

blunted affect

flat affect

inappropriate affect

catatonia

waxy flexibility

prodromal phase

active phase

residual phase

disorganized schizophrenia

catatonic schizophrenia

paranoid schizophrenia

undifferentiated type

residual type

Type I schizophrenia

Type II schizophrenia

chromosomal mapping

dopamine hypothesis

amphetamine psychosis

dopamine antagonists

paleologic thought

schizophrenogenic mother

double-bind hypothesis

SAMPLE
MULTIPLE-CHOICE
QUESTIONS

1. Schizophrenic people often have the symptom called loose associations. This symptom is a disturbance of:
   a. perception
   b. psychomotor behavior
   c. the form of thought
   d. the content of thought

2. The most common type of hallucination in schizophrenia is:
   a. visual
   b. auditory
   c. tactile
   d. olfactory

3. The term "catatonia" refers to which area of disturbance in schizophrenia?
   a. volition
   b. sense of self
   c. affect
   d. psychomotor behavior

4. The DSM-III-R specifies that a person must have shown continuous signs of schizophrenia for how long to receive a diagnosis of schizophrenia?
a. 1 month
b. 2 months
c. 6 months
d. 12 months

5. DSM-III-R suggests that the type of schizophrenia that is more likely to improve than the other forms is:
a. catatonic type
b. disorganized type
c. undifferentiated type
d. paranoid type

6. People who have a better premorbid adjustment, greater likelihood of improvement, and better response to the antipsychotic drugs are those who have:
a. Type I schizophrenia
b. Type II schizophrenia
c. prodromal schizophrenia
d. residual schizophrenia

7. What kind of genetic studies are the most rigorous?
a. twin studies
b. adoption studies
c. family studies
d. second-order relative studies

8. The major biochemical abnormality currently being considered in connection with schizophrenia is:
a. an excess of dopamine
b. a deficit of dopamine
c. an excess of phenothiazines
d. a deficit of phenothiazines

9. The double-bind hypothesis of the development of schizophrenia is concerned with:
a. substance abuse
b. communication
c. sexual stages
d. parental discipline

10. In Lidz's scheme of family structure, families in which the spouses are in open conflict are said to exhibit:
a. marital schism
b. marital skew
c. enmeshment
d. homeostasis

SAMPLE
SHORT-ANSWER
QUESTIONS

1. People who lose contact with reality are said to have a(n) _____.

2. The person who originated the name "schizophrenia" was _____.

3. A person who believes that a commercial on television is referring to him or her is experiencing a delusion of _____.

4. Schizophrenics frequently make up words that have meaning only to them. The made-up words are called _____.

5. A perception that occurs in the absence of external stimuli is called a(n) _____.

6. The tendency of some schizophrenics to maintain a posture in which they were placed by someone else is called _____.

7. What are the three typical phases of schizophrenia?

    _____
    _____
    _____

8. In the third phase of schizophrenia, the patient returns to the level of functioning of which previous phase?

    _____

9. For the diagnosis of schizophrenia, DSM-III-R requires that the person show continuous signs of schizophrenia for 6 months and that during this period the person display major symptoms during an active phase lasting at least _____.

10. The most prominent symptom of schizophrenia is _____.

11. Symptoms that represent pathological deficits and pathological excesses are called _____ and _____ symptoms, respectively.

12. There is some evidence that the negative symptoms of Type II schizophrenia are tied to _____.

13. The rate of schizophrenia in the general population is considered to be about _____ percent.

14. If both members of a pair of twins have a particular trait, they are said to be _____ for that trait.

15. Amphetamine psychosis is associated with an increase in the neurotransmitter _____ in the brain.

16. There is some evidence to suggest that an excess of dopamine activity may contribute only to _____ schizophrenia.

17. The structural abnormality of the brain identified in schizophrenic patients consists of enlarged _____.

18. The cold and domineering mother who is said to contribute to the development of schizophrenia is called a _____.

19. Laing considers the schizophrenic person's behavior as a(n) _____ process.

20. The cognitive view of schizophrenia is considered limited because it deals with only one aspect of schizophrenia, its _____.

EXPLANATIONS OF DIFFICULT MATERIAL

Research on biochemical and brain structure abnormalities have contributed to the understanding of schizophrenia; yet many people who display these abnormalities never develop schizophrenia. One hypothesis is that a biological abnormality predisposes a person to schizophrenia provided that other factors intervene. The biological abnormality could be genetic in origin or it could result from an environmental influence, such as a birth injury. The biological factor is *necessary* for the development of schizophrenia but is not *sufficient* in itself.

Some other factor must also be present if schizophrenia is to develop. Some candidates for this additional factor are parents who are in constant open conflict, or have difficulty communicating, or are extremely critical of and overinvolved with their children. Thus, a child who had the predisposing biological abnormality and whose parents behaved in one of these ways would be a candidate for schizophrenia. A child who had the same predisposing biological abnormality but was not exposed to the pathological parental behavior patterns would not develop schizophrenia. Children who lacked the predisposing biological abnormality would not develop schizophrenia whether or not their parents behaved in pathological ways. Children who were exposed to pathological behavior patterns might develop some other disorders or problems, but, according to this hypothesis, they would not develop schizophrenia because they lack the necessary predisposing biological abnormality. This hypothesis has not received significant research support, yet research does find family stresses in the backgrounds of most schizophrenic people.

ADDITIONAL READINGS

Andreason, N., & Flaum, M. (1991). Schizophrenia: The characteristic symptoms. *Schizophrenia Bulletin, 17,* 27–49.

Asaad, G., & Shapiro, B. (1986). Hallucinations: Theoretical and clinical overview. *American Journal of Psychiatry, 143,* 1088–1097.

Berquier, A., & Ashton, R. (1991). A selective review of possible neurological etiologies of schizophrenia. *Clinical Psychology Review, 11,* 645–661.

Bradbury, T. N., & Miller, G. A. (1985). Season of birth in schizophrenia: A review of evidence, methodology, and etiology. *Psychological Bulletin, 98, 569–595.*

Goldstein, M. J. (1987). Psychosocial issues. *Schizophrenia Bulletin, 13,* 157–171.

Goldstein, W. N. (1983). DSM-III and the diagnosis of schizophrenia. *American Journal of Psychiatry, 37,* 168–181.

Harrow, M., & Westermeyer, J. F. (1987). Process-reactive dimension and outcome for narrow concepts of schizophrenia. *Schizophrenia Bulletin, 13,* 361–368.

Hoenig, J. (1983). The concept of schizophrenia: Kraepelin-Bleuler-Schneider. *British Journal of Psychiatry, 142,* 547–556.

Keith, S. J., & Matthews, S. M. (1991). The diagnosis of schizophrenia: A review of onset and duration issues. *Schizophrenia Bulletin, 17,* 51–67.

Meltzer, H. Y. (1987). Biological studies in schizophrenia. *Schizophrenia Bulletin, 13,* 77–111.

ANSWER KEY

Multiple-Choice Questions:

1c, 2b, 3d, 4c, 5d, 6a, 7b, 8a, 9b, 10a.

Short-Answer Questions:

1. psychosis
2. Eugen Bleuler
3. reference
4. neologisms
5. hallucination
6. waxy flexibility
7. prodromal, active, residual
8. prodromal
9. one week
10. paranoid delusions
11. negative; positive
12. structural abnormalities (or enlarged ventricles) of the brain
13. 1
14. concordant
15. dopamine
16. Type I
17. ventricles
18. schizophrenogenic mother
19. constructive (or positive)
20. delusions

CHAPTER 16

TREATMENTS FOR SCHIZOPHRENIA

CHAPTER OVERVIEW

During the first half of the 20th century, treatment for
schizophrenic patients consisted of custodial care and physical
restraint in large *state hospitals.* In these circumstances
patients developed additional symptoms, most commonly an
extreme deterioration known as *social breakdown syndrome.*
In the 1950s humanistic theorists proposed to counter these
effects of institutionalization by the introduction of *milieu
therapy,* an approach in which patients were treated as persons
capable of running their own lives. These programs vary in
details and in effectiveness. In general they are less effective
than *token economy programs,* in which patients who behave
in accordance with an established set of standards are
rewarded with tokens that they can exchange for things and
opportunities they want. Some such programs incorporate a
response cost, or deduction of tokens for inappropriate
behavior. Some institutions have *leveled programs,* each with
its own set of target behaviors, through which patients can
progress until they are ready for discharge.

The *neuroleptic drugs* or antipsychotic drugs, also introduced
in the 1950s, have been shown to reduce the positive
symptoms of schizophrenia (such as delusions and
hallucinations) more effectively than they do the negative
symptoms (such as flat affect and motor retardation).
Unfortunately, they also produce such unwanted

extrapyramidal effects as *Parkinsonian symptoms, dystonia, akathisia,* and *tardive dyskinesia.*

Psychotherapy is sometimes helpful in conjunction with antipsychotic drugs, especially during the later stages of the disorder. Active insight therapists have greater success than the more passive therapists who do not set limits for their patients or offer them guidance. *Social therapy* (or *sociotherapy*) has been found to help keep patients out of the hospital. These patients receive help in self-management, problem solving, decision making, and the development of social skills; some sociotherapists even help patients find jobs, housing, and financial assistance. *Family therapists* help schizophrenic patients cope with the pressures of family life and offer guidance to other family members.

Under the policy of *deinstitutionalization*, begun in the 1950s, patients in state mental hospitals were to be released to receive care in *community mental health centers*. Hundreds of thousands of patients have been released, but there are still not enough community centers to serve them. A recent trend is short-term hospitalization followed by a program of *aftercare* in the community. This approach has been found more effective than long-term hospitalization in reducing symptoms and preventing relapses. Some communities offer *day centers* or *day hospitals*, where patients receive care during the day; they then go home for the night. The success of such programs may depend on the quality and type of care provided and on the availability of *halfway houses* staffed by *paraprofessionals*, where patients live as responsible adults but receive support and help. Many people recovering from schizophrenia receive occupational training in a *sheltered workshop*.

Effective community programs can help schizophrenic people recover, but less than half of all schizophrenic people receive adequate services, largely because not enough services are available and those that are provided are poorly coordinated. As a consequence, many released patients become homeless and go through repeated cycles of hospitalization, release, and readmission. The National Institute of Mental Health and various interest groups are pressing for more and better community care for schizophrenic people.

KEY TERMS

state hospitals

social breakdown syndrome

milieu therapy

token economy programs

response cost

leveled programs

neuroleptic drugs

extrapyramidal effects

social therapy (sociotherapy)

family therapists

deinstitutionalization

community mental health center

aftercare

day centers (day hospitals)

halfway houses

paraprofessionals

sheltered workshop

SAMPLE MULTIPLE-CHOICE QUESTIONS

1. Two institutional interventions developed in the 1950s were:
   a. insight therapy and milieu therapy
   b. milieu therapy and token economy programs
   c. token economy programs and group therapy
   d. insight therapy and group therapy

2. Research on token economy programs indicates that the tokens awarded for performance of a task are most effective when they are given:
a. immediately before the task is performed
b. immediately after the task is performed
c. some tokens before the task is performed and some afterward
d. at any time; all arrangements are essentially of equal effectiveness

3. When Paul and Lentz investigated institutional programs, they found that the most effective treatment program was:
a. milieu therapy
b. custodial care
c. token economy program
d. all were of essentially equal effectiveness

4. May found that the single most effective intervention for schizophrenic patients was:
a. antipsychotic drugs
b. psychodynamic therapy
c. milieu therapy
d. electroconvulsive therapy

5. Which of the extrapyramidal effects of the antipsychotic drugs is generally irreversible?
a. Parkinsonian symptoms
b. dystonia
c. akathisia
d. tardive dyskinesia

6. Psychotherapy can be useful in the treatment of schizophrenia:
a. in the early stage of the disorder
b. after the active symptoms have been reduced
c. both a and b
d. neither a nor b

7. A major feature of social therapy or sociotherapy is:
a. problem solving
b. a focus on the future
c. self-disclosure
d. group exercises

8. When the progress of schizophrenic patients in Canada and the United States was compared, it was found that on several variables:
   a. the Canadian program was superior
   b. the U.S. program was superior
   c. the two programs were essentially of equal effectiveness

9. Among the inadequacies of community treatment are:
   a. poorly trained mental health staff
   b. poor coordination of services
   c. both a and b
   d. neither a nor b

10. Patients who do not require hospitalization but cannot live alone or with their families are likely candidates for:
   a. shelters
   b. halfway houses
   c. day hospitals
   d. none of the above

SAMPLE SHORT-ANSWER QUESTIONS

1. The social breakdown syndrome is a pattern of deterioration resulting from _____.

2. Token economy programs are based on _____ principles.

3. Milieu therapy is based on _____ principles.

4. In a token economy program, target behaviors are selected for which the patients are to be

   _____.

5. Getting patients to make the transition from a hospital program to community living is a problem for the

   _____.

6. Three methods for facilitating the transfer from a hospital token economy program to life outside the hospital are:

   _____

   _____

   _____

153

7. Three therapies for schizophrenia initiated in the 1950s are: _____

    _____

    _____

8. Antipsychotic drugs are also called _____ drugs.

9. Antipsychotic drugs appear to be more effective with the (positive? negative?) symptoms of schizophrenia.

    _____

10. Four extrapyramidal effects of the antipsychotic drugs are: _____

    _____

    _____

    _____

11. Some of the unwanted effects of the antipsychotic drugs are called Parkinsonian symptoms because they resemble the symptoms of _____.

12. "Akathisia" refers to symptoms of _____.

13. Research suggests that therapists who are more successful with schizophrenic patients tend to take a more (active? passive?) role with the patient.

    _____

14. Family support groups have been developed to come to the aid of the _____ of schizophrenic patients.

15. The movement of large numbers of schizophrenic and other chronic mental patients from state hospitals into the community is referred to as

    _____.

16. The community approach advocates short-term hospitalization followed by a posthospitalization program of_____.

17. Partial hospitalization programs offer services at facilities called _____.

18. Residences for people who do not require hospitalization but cannot live alone or with their family are called _____.

19. A sheltered workshop offers _____ training.

20. A sizeable number of schizophrenic patients released from mental hospitals have become _____ .

EXPLANATIONS OF DIFFICULT MATERIAL

The impact of the antipsychotic drugs on the treatment of schizophrenia has been impressive. Carefully designed research has shown these drugs to be beneficial in reducing the symptoms of schizophrenic patients. It is also clear that antipsychotic drugs do not represent a cure for schizophrenia. If the drug is withdrawn, the symptoms often return. Also, as expected, the drugs are not effective with all patients. Some patients, probably a minority, receive little or no benefit from these drugs. It is the positive symptoms of schizophrenia that tend to respond to antipsychotic drugs; the drugs tend to have little or no effect on the negative symptoms, which are not as florid as the positive symptoms but nevertheless are extremely disabling.

Many or most schizophrenic people have problems functioning in occupational and social roles. These deficits do not appear to be altered by antipsychotic drugs. It seems clear that something more than antipsychotic drugs is needed to rehabilitate these patients. The teaching of social, problem solving, and occupational skills appears to have a place in any program designed to help schizophrenia patients learn to function in the community. The contribution of the antipsychotic drugs, impressive though it is, seems not to match that of the antianxiety and antidepressant drugs in helping the patients for whom they were developed lead normal lives. Many schizophrenic patients have behavioral deficits that cannot be changed by drugs.

ADDITIONAL READINGS

Backer, T. E., & Richardson, D. (1989). Building bridges: Psychologists and the families of the mentally ill. *American Psychologist, 44,* 546–550.

Bellak, A. S. (1986). Schizophrenia: Behavior therapy's forgotten child. *Behavior Therapy, 17,* 199–214.

Bellak, A. S. (Ed.) (1984). *Schizophrenia: Treatment, management, and rehabilitation.* Orlando: Grune & Stratton.

Carone, B. J., Harrow, M., & Westermeyer, J. F. (1991). Posthospital course and outcome in schizophrenia. *Archives of General Psychiatry, 48,* 247–253.

Carpenter, W. T., Jr. (1986). Thoughts on the treatment of schizophrenia. *Schizophrenia Bulletin, 12,* 527–539.

Davis, J. M., Schaffer, C. B., Killian, G. A., Kinard, C., & Chan, C. (1980). Important issues in the drug treatment of schizophrenia. *Schizophrenia Bulletin, 6,* 70–87.

Halford, W. K., & Hayes, R. (1991). Psychological rehabilitation of chronic schizophrenic patients: Recent findings on social skills training and family psychoeducation. *Clinical Psychology Review, 11,* 23–44.

Kane, J. M. (1987). Treatment of schizophrenia. *Schizophrenia Bulletin, 13,* 133–156.

Schooler, C., & Spohn, H. E. (1982). Social dysfunction and treatment failure in schizophrenia. *Schizophrenia Bulletin, 8,* 85–98.

ANSWER KEY

Multiple-Choice Questions:

1b, 2b, 3c, 4a, 5d, 6b, 7a, 8a, 9b, 10b.

Short-Answer Questions:

1. institutionalization
2. behavioral (or operant conditioning)
3. humanistic
4. rewarded (or reinforced)
5. token economy program
6. social reinforcements; partial reinforcement schedule; fading
7. milieu therapy; token economy; antipsychotic drugs
8. neuroleptic
9. positive
10. Parkinsonian symptoms; dystonia; akasthesia; tardive dyskinesia
11. Parkinson's disease
12. restlessness and agitation
13. active
14. relatives
15. deinstitutionalization
16. aftercare
17. day centers (or day hospitals)
18. halfway houses
19. occupational
20. homeless

CHAPTER 17

PERSONALITY DISORDERS

CHAPTER OVERVIEW

People with *personality disorders* display rigid and maladaptive patterns of behavior, perception, and emotion that harm their social and work lives and cause them distress. DSM-III-R recognizes eleven personality disorders, which it groups into three clusters. In *Cluster A* are the schizoid, paranoid, and schizotypal personality disorders, characterized by odd or eccentric traits. *Cluster B* consists of the antisocial, narcissistic, histrionic, and borderline personality disorders, all characterized by highly emotional and erratic behavior. The *Cluster C* disorders—the dependent, passive-aggressive, obsessive compulsive, and avoidant personality disorders—are distinguished by pervasive anxiety.

Theodore Millon proposes that the simplest way to understand anyone's personality is to understand the types of reinforcements the person typically seeks (positive or negative), their usual sources (the self or others), and the strategies used to obtain them (active or passive).

People with an *antisocial personality disorder* (or *psychopathy* or *sociopathy*) are unreliable, indifferent to others, dishonest, and given to destructive, often illegal behavior. They actively pursue pleasure and depend on themselves to attain it. Both biological and environmental factors may play roles in the development of this disorder, which does not yield to any known treatment.

People with a *narcissistic personality disorder* are absorbed in fantasies of fame, beauty, or success. Their interest in other people is focused on what others can do to help them attain their goals. They are easily hurt and discouraged. They seek pleasure, but do so passively and depend on themselves to attain it. Parental overindulgence may account for this disorder, which may be helped by long-term psychodynamic therapy and by social skills training.

People with a *histrionic personality disorder* display dramatic but shallow emotionality, demand constant attention, and are typically manipulative. They actively try to avoid pain, and depend on themselves to escape it. Both biological and environmental factors may contribute to this disorder. Antidepressant drugs are helpful in controlling the depression that often accompanies it.

People with a *dependent personality disorder* are so dependent on others and so needy of reassurance that they demean themselves to please others and even submit to abuse. Such people try to avoid pain by passively depending on others. Any physical or social deficit, real or imagined, may set the stage for the development of this disorder, which may benefit from therapy stressing training in social skills and assertiveness.

People with *passive-aggressive personality disorder* try to control other people indirectly. They are typically moody, skeptical, obstinate, and resentful. They try to avoid psychological pain by a covert form of aggression against people they see as threatening to their control. Biological factors may play some role in this disorder, but its development seems to depend more on family influences. Social skills and assertiveness training may be of benefit to these individuals.

People with an *obsessive compulsive personality disorder* are so concerned with doing everything perfectly that their work and their relationships suffer. They passively try to avoid pain, depending now on themselves, now on other people in their efforts to escape it. Both biological and family factors may figure in the development of this disorder. Social skills training, relaxation training, and cognitive techniques may be helpful to these people, but they are generally so fearful of change that they resist therapy.

Although people with an *avoidant personality disorder* yearn for social ties, they avoid relationships because they fear rejection. These people passively try to avoid pain but are unable to obtain reinforcement from either themselves or others. Biological vulnerability to social stimuli may develop into an avoidant personality disorder under the stress of rejection in childhood. Antianxiety drugs or biofeedback techniques may permit other therapies, such as desensitization, assertiveness and social skills training, and cognitive therapy, to reduce these patients' avoidant behavior.

People with *schizoid personality disorder* have no interest in other people and prefer to be alone. These people, too, passively avoid pain but are unable to obtain reinforcement from any source. Abnormal activity of the neurotransmitter dopamine seems to make these people oversensitive to stimulation and to trigger efforts to avoid it, which may be reinforced by childhood trauma. Given these people's resistance to any form of intimacy, it is difficult for a therapist to establish a relationship of trust, and no known drugs seem to benefit these patients.

People with a *paranoid personality disorder* trust no one but themselves. They are defensive, react quickly to any perceived threat, and rarely establish close relationships. This disorder can be seen as an intensified antisocial, narcissistic, or compulsive personality disorder and may emerge when a person with one of those disorders is subjected to extraordinary stress at a critical developmental stage. These people rarely seek or cooperate with therapy. The therapist's best strategy is to form a *therapeutic alliance* with the patient, agreeing that the world is indeed a dangerous place in some ways at some times, so that the patient can then be helped to distinguish real threats from perceived ones.

People with a *borderline personality disorder* are extremely unstable, unsure of themselves and their values, and ambivalent about others. This disorder can be seen as an extension of the histrionic, dependent, or passive-aggressive personality disorder. These people are ambivalent about what kind of reinforcement they prefer, about its source, and about whether to behave actively or passively to obtain it. The disorder appears to develop in childhood; the biological and environmental factors are not clearly understood. Therapy is difficult but may be helpful if a stable therapeutic environment can be established.

People with a *schizotypal personality disorder* are subject to delusions and hallucinations, blunted or inappropriate emotions, and other symptoms characteristic of schizophrenia, but in milder forms. It has been seen as a nonpsychotic variant of schizophrenia and as an extension of the avoidant and schizoid personality disorders. These people have great difficulty receiving any kind of reinforcement from any source. Biological and psychosocial factors appear to intertwine in this disorder. It can be helped by psychotherapy that emphasizes social skills training and assertiveness training.

DSM-III-R assigns "provisional" status to the sadistic and self-defeating personality disorders, pending further investigation. People with a *sadistic personality disorder* enjoy hurting other people physically and emotionally; they seek to control them and to limit their freedom. Their perceptions of pleasure and pain are so distorted that they receive pleasure by inflicting pain.

People with a *self-defeating personality disorder* habitually sabotage their own chances for happiness and success. They alienate other people either by demanding too much of them or by being too self-sacrificing. Their perceptions are so distorted that they accept suffering passively rather than avoid it.

KEY TERMS

antisocial personality disorder (psychopathy, sociopathy)

narcissistic personality disorder

histrionic personality disorder

dependent personality disorder

passive-aggressive personality disorder

obsessive compulsive personality disorder

avoidant personality disorder

schizoid personality disorder

paranoid personality disorder

therapeutic alliance

borderline personality disorder

schizotypal personality disorder

sadistic personality disorder

self-defeating personality disorder

SAMPLE
MULTIPLE-CHOICE
QUESTIONS

1. One difference between personality traits and
   personality disorders is that personality disorders:
   a. show consistency
   b. do not show consistency
   c. are maladaptive
   d. are usually not maladaptive

2. Personality disorders represent:
   a. Axis I disorders
   b. Axis II disorders
   c. both a and b
   d. neither a nor b

3. Antisocial personality disorder is also known as:
a. psychopathy
b. sociopathy
c. both a and b
d. neither a nor b

4. It is possible that an unconditional parental valuation of a child may lead to:
a. antisocial personality disorder
b. narcissistic personality disorder
c. dependent personality disorder
d. obsessive personality disorder

5. Extreme difficulty in making decisions is typical of:
a. antisocial personality disorder
b. histrionic personality disorder
c. narcissistic personality disorder
d. dependent personality disorder

6. Individuals who are so perfectionistic that they may be unable to complete tasks are most likely to fit which category of personality disorder?
a. passive-aggressive
b. histrionic
c. dependent
d. obsessive compulsive

7. The histrionic personality disorder resembles which of the following disorders?
a. somatization disorder
b. conversion disorder
c. factitious disorder
d. dysthymic disorder

8. If a drug were used in the treatment of the avoidant personality disorder, it would most likely be:
a. an antidepressant drug
b. an antipsychotic drug
c. an antianxiety drug
d. none of the above

9. Which of the personality disorders are much more severe than the others?
a. paranoid, borderline, schizotypal
b. antisocial, schizoid, avoidant
c. antisocial, paranoid, passive-aggressive
d. avoidant, passive-aggressive, borderline

10. Which two personality disorders occur more frequently in men than in women?
   a. antisocial and schizoid
   b. schizoid and paranoid
   c. paranoid and avoidant
   d. antisocial and obsessive compulsive

SAMPLE SHORT-ANSWER QUESTIONS

1. Characteristic patterns of behavior, perception, and emotion are known as _____.

2. Personality disorders usually become apparent by what developmental stage or age period?

3. The DSM-III-R includes in Cluster A personality disorders that are characterized by odd or eccentric qualities. Which three personality disorders are included in Cluster A?

   _____
   _____
   _____

4. Cluster C personality disorders share pervasive anxiety and fearfulness. List the four disorders included in Cluster C. _____

   _____
   _____
   _____

5. If one wishes to understand an individual's personality, it is helpful to understand the types of _____ that the person typically seeks.

6. Sources of reinforcement may be _____ or _____.

7. People who have a lifelong history of misconduct are most likely to fit the category of _____ personality disorder.

8. Is the source of reinforcement for the antisocial personality disorder self or others?

   _____

9. An exceedingly strong need to avoid boredom and
    emotional emptiness is typical of the _____
    personality disorder.

10. Deficient physical stature or impaired health may
    contribute to the development of the _____
    personality disorder.

11. Is the passive-aggressive personality disorder more a
    function of biological or of learning factors?

    _____

12. Is the obsessive compulsive personality disorder
    characterized by positive or negative reinforcement?

13. The self-defeating personality disorder resembles what
    two Axis I disorders?

    _____
    _____

14. The avoidant personality disorder is characterized by a
    fear of _____.

15. People with a schizoid personality disorder avoid social
    contact because they _____.

16. Which neurotransmitter is hypothesized to play a role in
    the development of the schizoid personality?

    _____

17. A therapeutic alliance should be established in the
    treatment of which personality disorder?

    _____

18. The hallmark of the borderline personality disorder is

    _____.

19. Which of the personality disorders has no source of
    reinforcement? _____

20. Which two personality disorders does DSM-III-R accord
    provisional status?

    _____
    _____

EXPLANATIONS OF DIFFICULT MATERIAL

Progress in the study of personality disorders has been hampered by the difficulty encountered by mental health professionals in reaching a consensus on the essential features of the various disorders. The relative lack of research on most of the personality disorders may reflect problems concerning the classification of this group of disorders. It is important to note that tentative defining criteria were formulated earlier for the antisocial personality disorder than for the other personality disorders. Also, and not surprisingly, the antisocial personality disorder, in contrast to the other personality disorders, has been studied quite extensively by a variety of research approaches. The remaining personality disorders appear now to be recognized, at least tentatively, as broad problem areas.

It is interesting to note, however, that two personality disorders are recognized only provisionally. Some of the current categories may change. Meaningful research on the specific personality disorders has been greatly facilitated by DSM-III-R's establishment of categories with defining criteria. Studies of the reliability and validity of the categories can now be conducted. Also, the overlap of the defining criteria of the several personality disorders can be determined. Only in this systematic empirical way can scientific progress be made toward understanding the personality disorders.

ADDITIONAL READINGS

Drake, R. E., & Vaillant, G. E. (1985). A validity study of Axis II of DSM-III. *American Journal of Psychiatry, 142,* 553–558.

Grove, W. M., & Tellegen, A. (1991). Problems in the classification of personality disorders. *Journal of Personality Disorders, 5,* 31–41.

Hare, R. D., & Schalling, D. (Eds.) (1978). *Psychopathic behavior: Approaches to research.* New York: Wiley.

Kass, F., Spitzer, R. L., & Williams, J. B. W. (1983). An empirical study of sex bias in the diagnostic criteria of DSM-III Axis II personality disorders. *American Psychologist, 38,* 799–801.

Lion, J. R. (Ed.) (1986). *Personality disorders: Diagnosis and management.* Malabar, Fla.: Robert F. Kreiger.

Lively, W. J. (1991). Classifying personality disorders: Ideal types, prototypes, or dimensions. *Journal of Personality Disorders, 5,* 52–59.

Loranger, A. W., Susman, V. L., Oldham, J. M., & Russakoff,

L. M. (1987). The personality disorder examination: A preliminary report. *Journal of Personality Disorders, 1,* 1–13.

Stangl, D., Pfohl, B., Zimmerman, M., Bowers, W., & Corenthal, R. (1985). A structured interview for the DSM-III personality disorders: A preliminary report. *Archives of General Psychiatry, 42, 591–596.*

Widiger, T. A., & Shea, T. (1991). Differentiation of Axis I and Axis II disorders. *Journal of Abnormal Psychology, 100, 399–406.* Wiggins, J. S., & Pincus, A. L. (1989). Conceptualizations of personality disorders and dimensions. *Psychological Assessment: A Journal of Consulting and Clinical Psychology, 1, 305–316.*

ANSWER KEY

Multiple-Choice Questions:

1c, 2b, 3c, 4b, 5d, 6d, 7a, 8c, 9a, 10d.

Short-Answer Questions:

1. personality traits
2. adolescence
3. schizoid, paranoid, schizotypal
4. dependent, passive-aggressive, obsessive compulsive, avoidant
5. reinforcements
6. others; oneself
7. antisocial
8. others
9. histrionic
10. dependent
11. learning
12. negative
13. sexual masochism, depressive disorder
14. rejection
15. prefer to be alone
16. dopamine
17. paranoid
18. instability
19. schizotypal
20. sadistic, self-defeating

CHAPTER 18

DISSOCIATIVE DISORDERS

CHAPTER OVERVIEW

Memory provides people with continuity and *identity*. People with dissociative disorders undergo significant changes in their memory or identity. Those with *psychogenic amnesia* are unable to recall important personal information and events. The most common type is *localized* (or *circumscribed*) *amnesia*, a forgetting of everything that happened during a limited time period, which begins with a traumatic event. People with *selective amnesia* forget some but not all events during the *amnestic episode*. People with *generalized amnesia* forget events extending from the traumatic event into the past; they may even forget who they are. In *continuous amnesia* the forgetting is ongoing, so that nothing that happens in the present is remembered.

People with *psychogenic fugue* physically flee during the amnestic episode and assume a new identity. Usually the episode is brief, but it can be quite extensive. The end usually comes abruptly.

A person with *multiple personality disorder* has two or more subpersonalities that alternate; usually one of them is dominant. Nearly all such people have been physically abused in early childhood. The subpersonalities may have *mutually amnestic relationships* (they are unaware of each other) or they may display *mutually cognizant patterns*. The most common pattern is a *one-way amnestic relationship*: some personalities are aware of the others but are not recognized by them. Those that are aware are *co-conscious personalities*. The various personalities have their own names, characteristics, vital statistics, abilities and preferences, and even physiological responses. Multiple personality disorder is relatively rare but its incidence appears to be increasing, perhaps because more clinicians now recognize it. Psychodynamic theorists regard the dissociative disorders as instances of extreme repression of childhood abuse. Yet many children are abused and few develop a dissociative disorder. Behaviorists attribute the disorders to operant conditioning: the reinforcement of relief from anxiety found in temporary forgetting of a traumatic event leads to total forgetting. Both of these explanations depend solely on case histories, and the behavioral explanation does not account for multiple personalities.

Research has established that what is learned when a person is in a particular state or situation is best remembered when the person is returned to the same state or situation. Some theorists believe that such *state-dependent learning* may explain the dissociative disorders. Other theorists point to *hypnotic amnesia*—amnesia produced by suggestion under hypnosis—as suggesting that the dissociative disorders are forms of *self-hypnosis*.

Many theorists regard psychodynamic therapy, with its emphasis on recovery of repressed material, as the most appropriate treatment for psychogenic amnesia and fugue. Another common treatment, sometimes in conjunction with psychodynamic therapy, is *hypnotic therapy (hypnotherapy)*. These approaches, cognitive and drug therapies, and even assertiveness training have been used to treat multiple personality disorder, but integration of the various personalities is usually difficult.

Depersonalization disorder differs from the other dissociative disorders in that it is one's body or mental functioning from which one feels dissociated. In a phenomenon called *doubling*, such people may feel that their mind is floating above their body, yet they are aware that their perceptions are distorted. The distortions may extend to the sense of smell or touch or to the perception of time or space. In the phenomenon of *derealization*, they may feel that the external world, too, is unreal or distorted. The disorder occurs primarily in young people who experience severe stress. Psychodynamic theorists view it as a defense mechanism. Cognitive theorists point to the experiences of persons subjected to *sensory deprivation* as evidence that the disorder stems from excessive attention to one's body processes and thoughts. No treatment approach has been clearly effective.

KEY TERMS

memory

identity

psychogenic amnesia

localized (circumscribed) amnesia

selective amnesia

amnestic episode

generalized amnesia

continuous amnesia

psychogenic fugue

multiple personality disorder

mutually amnestic relationship

mutually cognizant patterns

one-way amnestic relationship

co-conscious subpersonalities

repression

state-dependent learning

hypnotic amnesia

self-hypnosis

hypnotic therapy (hypnotherapy)

depersonalization disorder

doubling

derealization

sensory deprivation

SAMPLE
MULTIPLE-CHOICE
QUESTIONS

1. Some theorists reject the inclusion of which disorder
    among the dissociative disorders?
    a. psychogenic amnesia
    b. psychogenic fugue
    c. multiple personality disorder
    d. depersonalization disorder

2. Which type of psychogenic amnesia is the most
    common?
    a. localized
    b. selective
    c. generalized
    d. continuous

3. Which of the following is likely to be forgotten by
    people who have psychogenic amnesia?
    a. how to drive a car
    b. how to read and write
    c. their own names
    d. all of the above

4. Psychogenic amnesia and fugue episodes:
    a. tend to end abruptly
    b. have a tendency to recur
    c. both a and b
    d. neither a nor b

5. Most cases of multiple personality disorder are first
    diagnosed in:
    a. late adolescence or young adulthood
    b. middle age
    c. upper age range
    d. all ages about equally

6. The various personalities in a multiple personality
    disorder can differ with respect to:
    a. age and sex
    b. personality
    c. abilities and preferences
    d. all of the above

7. The psychodynamic and behavioral explanations of dissociative disorders are similar in the sense that both consider the disorders to be:
   a. due to repression
   b. precipitated by traumatic experiences
   c. both a and b
   d. neither a nor b

8. The principles of state-dependent learning have been proposed to account for:
   a. psychogenic amnesia
   b. psychogenic fugue
   c. multiple personality disorder
   d. all of the above

9. Most cases of psychogenic amnesia and fugue recover:
   a. with psychodynamic therapy
   b. with drug therapy
   c. with systematic desensitization
   d. spontaneously without therapy

10. A sensation called doubling occurs in which of the dissociative disorders?
    a. psychogenic amnesia and fugue
    b. multiple personality disorder
    c. depersonalization disorder
    d. all of the above

SAMPLE SHORT-ANSWER QUESTIONS

1. People with dissociative disorder experience a significant alteration in their _____ or _____.

2. List the four types of psychogenic amnesia.
   _____
   _____
   _____
   _____

3. Which is the least common of the four types of psychogenic amnesia? _____

4. Psychogenic amnesia is often precipitated by extreme _____.

171

5. When a psychogenic amnesia episode involves travel to a different location, it is called psychogenic

    _____.

6. The additional personalities shown by an individual with multiple personality disorder are called

    _____.

7. Recent evidence suggests that multiple personality disorder is _____ common than it was once believed to be.

8. When subpersonalities are well aware of each other, they are said to be _____.

9. When subpersonalities have no awareness of each other, they are said to be _____.

10. Research has shown that the brain activity patterns of the various subpersonalities of people with multiple personality disorder are (similar? different?).

    _____

11. The evidence (supports? does not support?) the notion that cases of multiple personality disorders are iatrogenic.

    _____

12. Psychodynamic theorists explain dissociative disorders on the basis of extreme _____.

13. Behaviorists consider dissociation to be a response acquired through _____.

14. Our tendency to remember something best when we are in the same state or situation as we were in when we learned that material is called _____.

15. Some theorists have proposed that the dissociative disorders may represent a form of

    _____.

16. The drugs sodium amobarbital and sodium pentobarbital are used to help amnesia patients regain

    _____.

17. The experiences of subjects in sensory deprivation experiments are cited to support which view of depersonalization disorders?

_____

18. The feeling that the external world is unreal and strange is referred to as _____.

19. Evidence indicates that approximately _____ percent of adolescents and young people occasionally experience symptoms of depersonalization and derealization.

20. Psychodynamic theorists view depersonalization as an extreme _____.

EXPLANATIONS OF DIFFICULT MATERIAL

Self-hypnosis has emerged as one of the more strongly supported explanations for the dissociative disorders. Two important findings are (1) a close association between the dissociative disorders and a history of traumatic or brutal childhood experiences and (2) evidence that people with multiple personality disorder appear to be highly susceptible to hypnosis and to be capable of hypnotic amnesia. The assumption is that these abused children used what could be called self-hypnosis as a means of coping with traumatic experiences. Two problems arise with this view of multiple personality disorder: some people with multiple personality disorder do not appear to have suffered serious abuse as children, and child abuse appears to be much more common than multiple personality disorder.

The answer to the first problem may be that these children *perceived* that they were subjected to psychological abuse, even though they may not have been abused physically. The second problem disappears if we assume that only a small proportion of victims of child abuse have learned self-hypnosis and resorted to it as a defense against their traumatic experiences. The self-hypnosis explanation may not be the final answer to the development of multiple personality disorder, yet it is not necessarily disproved by these apparent contradictions.

ADDITIONAL READINGS

Aalpoel, P. J., & Lewis, D. J. (1984). Dissociative disorders. In H. E. Adams & P. B. Sutker (Eds.), *Comprehensive handbook of psychopathology*. New York: Plenum.

Coons, P. M., & Milstein, V. (1986). Psychosexual disturbances in multiple personality: Characteristics, etiology, and treatment. *Journal of Clinical Psychiatry, 47,* 106–110.

Kaszniak, A. W., Nussbaum, P. D., Berren, M. R., & Santiago, J. (1988). Amnesia as a consequence of male rape: A case study. *Journal of Abnormal Psychology, 97,* 100–104.

Loftus, E. F., & Burns, T. E. (1982). Mental shock can produce retrograde amnesia. *Memory and Cognition, 10,* 318–323.

Schacter, D. L. (1986). Amnesia and crime: How much do we really know? *American Psychologist, 41,* 286–295.

Schacter, D. L., Wang, P. L., Tulving, E., & Freedman, M. (1982). Functional retrograde amnesia: A quantitative case study. *Neuropsychologia, 5,* 523–532.

Spanos, N. P., Weekes, J. R., & Bertrand, L. D. (1985). Multiple personality: A social psychological perspective. *Journal of Abnormal Psychology, 94,* 362–376.

Spiegel, D., & Cardena, E. (1991). Disintegrated experiences: The dissociative disorders revisited. *Journal of Abnormal Psychology, 100,* 366–378.

Steinbereg, M. (1991). The spectrum of depersonalization: Assessment and treatment. *Annual Review of Psychiatry, 10,* 223–247.

ANSWER KEY

Multiple-Choice Questions:

1d, 2a, 3c, 4a, 5a, 6d, 7b, 8c, 9d, 10c.

Short-Answer Questions:

1. memory; identity
2. localized, selective, generalized, continuous
3. continuous
4. stress
5. fugue
6. subpersonalities
7. more
8. mutually cognizant
9. mutually amnestic
10. different

11. does not support
12. repression
13. operant conditioning
14. state-dependent learning
15. self-hypnosis
16. lost memories
17. cognitive
18. derealization
19. 70
20. defense mechanism

CHAPTER 19

PROBLEMS OF CHILDHOOD AND ADOLESCENCE

CHAPTER OVERVIEW

Erik Erikson proposes that all people pass through eight stages of development, each with its own tasks and each marked by a particular "crisis," or turning point. Failure to master the tasks of one stage leads to pathology in the next. The task of stage 1, during the first year of life, is to develop a sense of trust. The child who fails to develop autonomy in stage 2, during the second year of life, feels shame and doubt, and may respond with either compulsive compliance or impulsive defiance. In stage 3, during the third or fourth year, children develop a sense of initiative. Those whose initiative is stifled may become paralyzed by guilt. During stage 4, which lasts from children's entrance into school until adolescence, they develop a sense of either industry or inferiority. During stage 5, which lasts through adolescence, those who fail to develop a sense of identity fall victim to role confusion. During stage 6, in early adulthood, people who fail to establish intimate relationships become isolated and may develop such psychological problems as irrational fears or depression. During stage 7, in middle adulthood, people ordinarily focus on the next generation. Those who fail to develop such generativity may fall prey to stagnation. The task of stage 8, in old age, is to integrate the insights one has gained so that one accepts both life and approaching death. Those who fail to achieve integrity may fall into despair.

Anxiety is common in childhood. Children with *separation anxiety disorder* become fearful whenever they are separated from a parent. The disorder sometimes takes the form of *school phobia*. Children with an *avoidant disorder* become very timid and withdrawn at any contact with strangers. *Overanxious disorder* is marked by inordinate fear or worry for at least 6 months. Behaviorists explain the childhood anxiety disorders as being the result of classical conditioning and treat them with desensitization and modeling techniques. Psychodynamic theorists attribute them to excessive repression and displacement and typically treat them with play therapy. Biological theorists point to physiological abnormalities.

Three kinds of *childhood depression* are recognized: acute, chronic, and masked. They are explained and treated in the same ways as adult depression.

Children with *oppositional defiant disorder* are frequently angry and rebellious. *Conduct disorder* is marked by greater aggression, cruelty, and destructiveness. Conduct disorders are usually attributed to family dysfunctioning, and a common approach is family intervention. Juvenile delinquents are generally institutionalized. Behavior therapy is sometimes effective.

Children with *attention-deficit hyperactivity disorder (ADHD)*, also called *hyperactivity* or *hyperkinesis,* are impulsive and overactive. It often coincides with conduct disorders. Biological factors are often suspected but none has been identified. Other theorists point to psychological factors such as stress. Most clinicians view hyperactivity as resulting from multiple interacting factors. Stimulant drugs are often prescribed. Operant conditioning treatments, alone or in conjunction with stimulants, have had some success. The effectiveness of self-instructional training is not yet certain.

Children with *functional enuresis* urinate in bed or in their pants. Psychodynamic theorists regard it as a symptom of a more general disorder. Family systems theorists attribute it to anxiety or hostility caused by disturbed family interactions. Behaviorists view it as a failure of toilet training. Treatment based on behavioral principles has had considerable success. *Functional encopresis,* or involuntary defecation, is less common. Explanations range from inadequate toilet training to stress. It has been successfully treated by medical and/or behavioral techniques and by family therapy.

The *specific developmental disorders* include *developmental arithmetic disorder, developmental expressive writing*

178

disorder, and *developmental reading disorder,* or *dyslexia.*
Language and speech disorders include *developmental articulation disorder,* which yields to speech therapy; *developmental expressive language disorder,* which usually disappears before adulthood; and *developmental receptive language disorder,* which may be a lifelong problem. The *developmental coordination disorder* also can be a lifelong problem. The causes of these disorders are unclear. According to the *perceptual deficit theory,* they result from problems in perceptual processing. The *academic instruction theory* attributes all but the coordination disorder to poor teaching. Behavioral techniques have been successful in reversing them.

The essential features of *autistic disorder (autism)* are unresponsiveness to others; language and communication deficits, such as *echolalia* and *pronominal reversal;* and deviant responses to the environment, such as *preservation of sameness, self-stimulatory behaviors,* and *self-injurious behaviors.* Some theorists attribute autism to disturbances in the ability to comprehend sounds; to stimulus overselectivity; and to inability to code information. Biological theorists link it to genetic factors, prenatal or birth difficulties, or organic brain dysfunctioning. Other theorists attribute the disorder to characteristics of the parents, family interactions, and stress; but research indicates that environmental factors do not cause autism. No treatment reverses the pattern, but these children may be helped to function better by drug therapy in conjunction with behavioral and educational approaches. Group homes are being established for autistic adolescents and adults.

People given a diagnosis of *mental retardation* have an IQ of 70 or lower, are deficient in adaptive functioning, and develop these symptoms before age 18. They learn slowly and have difficulties with memory and language. About 85 percent of these people are placed in the category of *mild retardation* (IQ 50–70). It has been linked primarily to genetic factors and a deprived environment. About 10 percent of retarded people function at a level of *moderate retardation* (IQ 35–49). The 5 percent in the category of *severe retardation* (IQ 20–34) can profit from some training but can work only in sheltered settings. The *profoundly retarded* (IQ < 20) require close supervision all of their lives, which may be short. Moderate, severe, and profound retardation are caused principally by biological factors, primarily chromosomal disorders *(Down syndrome),* metabolic disorders *(phenylketonuria* or *PKU* and *Tay-Sachs disease),* prenatal problems *(cretinism, fetal alcohol syndrome,* and the effects of rubella and syphilis), birth

179

complications (anoxia and extreme prematurity), and postnatal injuries and diseases. *Microencephaly* and *hydrocephalus* have multiple biological causes. Community residences have enabled some retarded people to live successfully in the community. Operant learning principles are employed in the education of retarded people. Many work in sheltered workshops.

KEY TERMS

separation anxiety disorder

avoidant disorder

overanxious disorder

childhood depression

oppositional defiant disorder

conduct disorder

attention-deficit hyperactivity disorder (ADHD)
  (hyperactivity, hyperkinesis)

functional enuresis

developmental expressive language disorder

developmental receptive language disorder

developmental coordination disorder

perceptual deficit theory

academic instruction theory

autistic disorder (autism)

mental retardation

mild retardation

functional encopresis

specific developmental disorders

developmental arithmetic disorder

developmental expressive writing disorder

developmental reading disorder (dyslexia)

developmental articulation disorder

moderate retardation

severe retardation

profound retardation

Down syndrome

phenylketonuria (PKU)

Tay-Sachs disease

cretinism

fetal alcohol syndrome

microencephaly

hydrocephalus

SAMPLE
MULTIPLE-CHOICE
QUESTIONS

1. In the first of Erikson's developmental stages the child needs to develop:
    a. trust
    b. autonomy
    c. initiative
    d. identity

2. Attention-deficit hyperactivity disorder is often seen in conjunction with:
    a. childhood depression
    b. childhood anxiety disorders
    c. conduct disorders
    d. autistic disorder

3. Specific developmental disorders are also known as:
    a. mental retardation
    b. hyperkinesis
    c. autistic disorders
    d. learning disabilities

4. Which of the following symptoms is considered of central importance to the autistic disorder?
   a. language and communication deficits
   b. deviant responses to the environment
   c. lack of responsiveness to others
   d. subaverage intellectual functioning

5. The speech peculiarity called echolalia is likely to occur in:
   a. mental retardation
   b. attention-deficit hyperactivity disorder
   c. autistic disorder
   d. all of the above

6. The onset of the autistic disorder occurs before what age?
   a. 1 year
   b. 3 years
   c. 6 years
   d. 12 years

7. Which of the following has been found in autistic children?
   a. higher rate of maternal rubella during pregnancy
   b. higher rate of birth complications
   c. both a and b
   d. neither a nor b

8. The largest proportion of all mentally retarded persons fall into which category?
   a. mild retardation
   b. moderate retardation
   c. severe retardation
   d. profound retardation

9. Phenylketonuria (PKU) is a genetic type of mental retardation caused by:
   a. a dominant gene
   b. recessive genes
   c. a chromosomal abnormality
   d. none of the above

10. Children who are affected with PKU can be prevented from developing mental retardation if they are:
    a. treated with Suproxin
    b. put on a special diet
    c. given a blood transfusion
    d. given high doses of Vitamin A

SAMPLE
SHORT-ANSWER
QUESTIONS

1. List the three forms of childhood anxiety disorders.

    _____

    _____

    _____

2. Which disorder is similar to but less severe than conduct disorder? _____

3. Critics of the penal system suggest that delinquency may best be dealt with by _____ programs.

4. The attention-deficit hyperactivity disorder (ADHD) is commonly called _____.

5. ADHD is more common in (boys? girls?).

    _____

6. What has been the most common approach to the treatment of ADHD? _____

7. Elimination disorders consist of which two specific disorders?

    _____

    _____

8. Developmental reading disorders are also known as _____.

9. The two leading explanations of specific developmental disorders are _____ and _____.

10. The prevalence of autism among the siblings of autistic children is (higher than? the same as?) the rate in the general population._____

11. Research has identified imbalances of which two neurotransmitters in autistic children?

    _____

    _____

12. List the three areas on which environmental and family views of autism have focused.

   _____
   _____
   _____

13. Two drugs that have been found useful in the treatment of autistic children are

   _____ and

   _____.

14. Behavioral treatment programs for autistic children typically involve the parents so that they

   _____.

15. DSM-III-R indicates that mental retardation involves subaverage intellectual functioning and impaired

   _____.

16. Three types of chromosomal aberrations can cause Down syndrome. List them.

   _____
   _____
   _____

17. A condition that leads to mental retardation and other serious problems as a result of the mother's abuse of alcohol during pregnancy is called

   _____.

18. Two early childhood diseases that can lead to mental retardation are _____ and

   _____.

19. In recent decades the focus of the treatment of mentally retarded persons has been on what is called

   _____.

20. The alternative to special education for mentally retarded children is _____.

EXPLANATION OF
DIFFICULT MATERIAL

DSM-III-R's criteria for the diagnosis of mental retardation are subaverage general intellectual functioning, associated impairment of adaptive behavior, and the appearance of these two indicators before the age of 18. These criteria were developed by the American Association on Mental Deficiency (AAMD) and adopted in DSM-III and DSM-III-R. It is important to understand the reasoning behind each of these criteria. It is reasonable that a measure of intellectual functioning be included and that standardized individually administered intelligence tests be used to measure this dimension. Despite criticisms of intelligence tests, they remain the most reliable and valid means to measure general intellectual functioning.

In almost all cases, intelligence test scores are more valid than the subjective judgments of clinicians, teachers, or parents. Impaired adaptive behavior also needs to be present for a diagnosis of mental retardation to be made. Thus if a child has subaverage intelligence but no impairment of adaptive behavior, that child is not mentally retarded. Similarly, if a child displays impaired adaptive behavior but is of average intelligence, that child is also not mentally retarded. Both of these children may have some problem, but it does not appear to be mental retardation. Therefore, a low IQ score that is not accompanied by impaired adaptive behavior indicates that the child's poor performance on the intelligence test must not be attributed to mental retardation.

The DSM-III-R definition serves to guard against such a misdiagnosis, since the diagnosis is not based on tested intelligence alone. The third item in the definition represents a decision to regard all people who display subaverage intellectual functioning and impaired adaptive behavior before age 18 as mentally retarded. Such deficits that originate after age 18 are referred to as organic mental syndrome and disorder.

ADDITIONAL READINGS

Balthazor, M. J., Wagner, R. K., & Pelham, W. F. (1991). The specificity of the effects of stimulant medication on classroom learning-related measures of cognitive processing for attention deficit disorder children. *Journal of Abnormal Child Psychology, 19,* 35–52.

Barkley, R. A. (1991). The ecological validity of laboratory and analogue assessment methods of ADHD symptoms. *Journal of Abnormal Child Psychology, 19,* 149–178.

Bouchard, T. J., & McGue, M. (1981). Familial studies of intelligence: A review. *Science, 212,* 1055–1059.

Campbell, S. B. (1990). *Behavior problems in preschool children: Clinical and developmental issues.* New York: Guilford.

Hersen, M., & Ollendick, T. (Eds.) (1989). *Handbook of child psychopathology* (2nd ed.). New York: Plenum.

Klein, R. G., & Last, C. G. (1989). *Anxiety disorders in children.* Newbury Park, Calif.: Sage.

Loeber, R., Green, S. M., & Lahey, B. B. (1990). Mental health professionals' perceptions of the utility of children, parents, and teachers as informants on child psychopathology. *Journal of Clinical Child Psychology, 19,* 136–143.

Lovaas, O. I. (1987). Behavioral treatment and normal educational and intellectual functioning in young autistic children. *Journal of Consulting and Clinical Psychology, 55,* 3–9.

Werry, J. S., Reeves, J. C., & Elkind, G. S. (1987). Attention deficit, conduct, oppositional, and anxiety disorders in children: I. A review of research of differentiating characteristics. *Journal of the American Academy of Child and Adolescent Psychiatry, 6,* 133–143.

Werry, J. S., & Wollersheim, J. P. (1989). Behavior therapy with children and adolescents: A twenty-year overview. *Journal of the American Academy of Child and Adolescent Psychiatry, 28,* 1–18.

Whelan, C. K., & Hanker, B. (1991). Therapies for hyperactive children: Comparisons, combinations, and compromises. *Journal of Consulting and Clinical Psychology, 59,* 126–137.

ANSWER KEY

Multiple-Choice Questions:

1a, 2c, 3d, 4c, 5c, 6b, 7c, 8a, 9b, 10b.

Short-Answer Questions:

1. separation anxiety disorder, avoidant disorder, and overanxious disorder
2. oppositional defiant disorder
3. prevention
4. hyperactivity or hyperkinesis

5. boys
6. stimulant drugs
7. enuresis, encopresis
8. dyslexia
9. perceptual deficit (or processing) theory; academic instruction theory
10. higher than
11. dopamine, serotonin
12. characteristics of parents, family interactions, stress
13. haloperidol; fenfluramine
14. may apply the techniques
15. adaptive behavior
16. trisomy 21, mosaicism, translocation
17. fetal alcohol syndrome
18. meningitis, encephalitis
19. normalization
20. mainstreaming

CHAPTER 20

PROBLEMS OF AGING

CHAPTER OVERVIEW

Adulthood, like childhood, is marked by developmental changes. *Early adulthood,* the years from about 22 to 40, is a period of high energy and stress. During *middle adulthood,* the years from 45 to 60, the slowing of biological functioning can produce stress. The period of transition between stages can be especially stressful. In the *early adult transition,* from age 17 to 22, people typically feel insecure and anxious. The *middle life transition,* from age 40 to 45, is even more stressful and is popularly referred to as the *midlife crisis*. The values and expectations of one's *cohort* may also be sources of stress.

Chronological age is not considered a true indicator of one's functional capacities. *Functional age* reflects biological, social, and psychological aspects of the aging process. *Biological age* is assessed by the functioning of vital organ systems. *Social age* reflects one's roles, habits, and behavior in comparison with those of other members of the same society. *Psychological age* reflects one's capacity to adapt one's behavior to the changing environment.

The *stress-and-coping model* suggests that people's ability to cope with stress depends on how they appraise the situation. If the *primary appraisal* results in a judgment that the situation is stressful, people then make a *secondary appraisal* to determine what to do about it. As the situation develops, they are likely to make *reappraisals*. All of these appraisals determine how they will react. Some people use *problem-focused strategies* to cope with difficulties, whereas others use *emotion-focused strategies*. Problem-focused strategies are found to be most effective in general, though emotion-focused strategies can sometimes be adaptive. Cognitive and behavioral therapies are helpful in efforts to alleviate many problems of the elderly.

The most common mental health problem among older people is depression. Antidepressant drugs must be carefully monitored because the metabolic rate slows with age. Cognitive-behavioral and brief psychodynamic therapies are frequently effective, especially in combination with drug therapy. Family and group therapies are sometimes helpful. ECT is used for patients who do not respond to other treatments. Psychoeducation programs can prevent depression from developing.

Anxiety often coincides with depression among the elderly. A cognitive-behavioral approach called *anxiety management techniques (AMT)*, which develops skills for controlling fear, is often preferred to anxiety drugs. Social skills training and psychodynamic appproaches are also used.

Dementia is an organic brain syndrome marked by significant cognitive impairment in memory, abstract thinking, and judgment; and other disturbances of higher cognitive functioning, such as impaired performance of psychomotor tasks; and noticeable personality changes. The most common form is *Alzheimer's disease*, which usually occurs after 65. Dysfunctioning progresses insidiously and there is no known cure. Structural changes in brain tissue are found at autopsy after death. *Multi-infarct dementia*, the second most common form of dementia, is caused by loss of blood flow to the brain during a stroke. This disease, too, is progressive, but the symptoms appear suddenly and only a limited portion of the brain is affected. *Pick's disease* is difficult to differentiate from Alzheimer's and appears to have a genetic component. *Jakob-Creutzfeldt disease* is accompanied by spasmodic movements and is caused by a slow-acting virus. *Huntington's chorea*, which starts with a movement disorder, is inherited through a chromosome other than a sex chromosome. The loss of motor control in *Parkinson's disease* is often accompanied by dementia.

Alzheimer's disease is widely thought to have a genetic basis, but other theories are being explored. Behavioral techniques can improve the quality of life for both patients and their caregivers. Support groups are also helpful for caregivers.

Alcohol and other forms of drug abuse decline after age 60, but they do affect substantial numbers of the elderly. Some older people misuse prescription drugs either intentionally or inadvertently.

The symptoms of schizophrenia are usually less severe among the elderly than among younger people. Delusional disorder increases slightly with age but is still rare. The mental health problems of older people can be significantly affected by their ethnicity, and clinicians must take patients' *ethnic group* into account when they diagnose and treat them.

The quality of long-term care provided for older adults varies widely. Loss of independence and the extreme expense of long-term-care facilities can cause depression and anxiety.

KEY TERMS

early adulthood

middle adulthood

early adult transition

middle life transition (midlife crisis)

cohorts

dementia

chronological age

functional age

biological age

social age

psychological age

stress-and-coping model

primary appraisal

secondary appraisal

reappraisals

problem-focused strategies

emotion-focused strategies

anxiety management techniques (AMT)

dementia

Alzheimer's disease

multi-infarct dementia

Pick's disease

Jakob-Creutzfeldt disease

Huntington's chorea

Parkinson's disease

ethnic group

SAMPLE
MULTIPLE-CHOICE
QUESTIONS

1. The capacity to adapt one's behavior to the changing environment is reflected in one's:
    a. psychological age
    b. biological age
    c. social age
    d. geophysical age

2. According to the stress-and-coping model, when people confront a potentially stressful situation, they evaluate whether the situation is irrelevant, positive, or stressful. This process is called:
    a. primary appraisal
    b. secondary appraisal
    c. general processing
    d. specific processing

3. Depression is best assessed in older adults by means of:
    a. a self-report questionnaire
    b. physiological measures
    c. a structured interview
    d. a behavioral checklist

4. Surveys suggest that the prevalence of anxiety disorders among elderly adults is:
    a. lower than among younger adults
    b. higher than among younger adults
    c. essentially the same as among younger adults

5. Dementia is an organic mental syndrome that is also known as:
    a. delirium
    b. mental retardation
    c. both a and b
    d. neither a nor b

6. The most common cause of dementia in the United
    States is:
    a. Huntington's chorea
    b. Parkinson's disease
    c. Tay-Sachs disease
    d. Alzheimer's disease

7. Huntington's chorea is known to be caused by:
    a. a recessive pattern of inheritance
    b. a dominant pattern of inheritance
    c. chronic use of alcohol
    d. a syphilitic infection

8. Which psychotic disorder increases slightly with age?
    a. schizophrenia
    b. obsessive compulsive disorder
    c. panic disorder
    d. delusional disorder

9. The term "double jeopardy" is applied to a person who
    is:
    a. old and physically handicapped
    b. old and with income below the poverty line
    c. an ethnic minority member with a physical handicap
    d. old and a member of an ethnic minority group

10. Among the elderly:
    a. abuse of both street and prescription drugs is high
    b. abuse of both street and prescription drugs is low
    c. abuse of street drugs is high and abuse of prescription
    drugs is low
    d. abuse of street drugs is low and abuse of prescription
    drugs is high

SAMPLE
SHORT-ANSWER
QUESTIONS

1. Erikson believes that possibilities for either growth or
    maladaptiveness are provided by all
    _____.

2. Groups of people born in the same year or time period
    are called _____.

3. The field concerned with the mental health of the
    elderly is _____.

194

4. What three aspects of aging are included in the concept of functional age?

   _____

   _____

   _____

5. The stress-and-coping model suggests that the key to coping is how one _____ a situation or event.

6. What two coping strategies are posited by the stress-and-coping model?

   _____

   _____

7. Because of the overlap of symptoms, an older person who is depressed may be diagnosed as having

   _____.

8. When antidepressant drugs are prescribed, older adults are often found to need a (lower? higher?) dosage than younger adults do. _____

9. Surveys suggest that the prevalence of anxiety disorders (increases? decreases?) with age. _____

10. If Alzheimer's disease occurs in middle age, rather than after the age of 65, it is called the _____ type.

11. The second most common type of dementia among the elderly is

    _____.

12. Multi-infarct dementia occurs more often in (men? women?).

    _____

13. Pick's disease is a rare progressive form of

    _____.

14. Two theories about the cause of Alzheimer's disease point to the functioning of which two neurotransmitters?

    _____

    _____

15. One recent development that offers help for the families of Alzheimer's victims is the _____ movement.

16. Caregiving is extremely difficult for the close relatives of _____ patients.

17. Two special concerns that clinicians must consider in connection with patients with dementia are _____and _____.

18. Older problem drinkers are often divided into two major categories: _____ and _____ abusers.

19. A patient's ethnicity should be taken into consideration because mental dysfunction may be related to _____.

20. The encouragement of lifelong participation in health maintenance programs should be supported by _____.

EXPLANATIONS OF DIFFICULT MATERIAL

The stress-and-coping model serves as a useful way to conceptualize the experience of stress throughout the life span. Its major concepts are primary appraisal, secondary appraisal, reappraisal, and coping. All three appraisal processes, especially primary appraisal, depend on the person's cognitive or internal representation of the situation. The process of perceiving stress, therefore, may be largely a matter of how a person evaluates that situation. People can differ greatly in their evaluations. Also, the way people decide to respond to a stressful situation depends heavily on the way they evaluate various possible coping efforts. A response that one person evaluates as an appropriate and efficient way of coping may be rejected by another person. The stress-and-coping model represents a strongly cognitive approach.

ADDITIONAL READINGS

Aronson, M. K. (Ed.) (1988). *Understanding Alzheimer's disease.* New York: Scribner's.
Carstensen, L. L., & Edelstein, B. A. (Eds.) (1988). *Handbook of clinical gerontology.* New York: Pergamon.
Fisher, J. E., & Carstensen, L. L. (1990). Behavioral management of the dementias. *Clinical Psychology Review, 10,* 611–629.

Heston, L. L., & White, J. A. (1991). *The vanishing mind: A practical guide to Alzheimer's disease and other dementias.* New York: W. H. Freeman.

Lezak, M. D. (1987). Norms for growing older. *Developmental Neuropsychology, 3,* 1–12.

Storandt, M., & VandenBos, G. R. (Eds.) (1989). *The adult years: Continuity and change.* Washington, D.C.: American Psychological Association.

Woodruff-Pak, D. S. (1988). *Psychology and aging.* Englewood Cliffs, N.J.: Prentice-Hall.

ANSWER KEY

Multiple-Choice Questions:

1a, 2a, 3c, 4a, 5d, 6d, 7b, 8d, 9d, 10d.

Short-Answer Questions:

1. developmental stages
2. cohorts
3. gerontology
4. biological, social, psychological
5. cognitively appraises (appraises)
6. problem-focused strategies; emotion-focused strategies
7. dementia (cognitive impairment)
8. lower
9. decreases
10. presenile
11. multi-infarct dementia
12. men
13. dementia
14. acetylcholine, L-glutamate
15. support group
16. Alzheimer's
17. the influence of ethnicity; the nursing home industry
18. early-onset; late-onset
19. discrimination
20. mental health professionals

CHAPTER 21

LAW, SOCIETY, AND THE MENTAL HEALTH PROFESSION

CHAPTER OVERVIEW

People who face trial for a criminal offense are presumed to be responsible for their actions and capable of participating in their defense in court. *Mental instability* is presumed to render one incapable in both respects. The courts judge defendants' mental stability but they are guided by the judgments of mental health professionals. Accused persons judged to be mentally unstable are subjected to *criminal commitment* to a mental institution. Persons found to be not guilty by reason of insanity at the time of the crime are committed for treatment until they improve enough to be released. Persons found to be mentally unstable at the time of their trial are committed for treatment until they are competent to stand trial. These judgments, too, are heavily influenced by mental health professionals.

For many years the courts relied on the *M'Naghten rule,* which specified that defendants who pleaded insanity must prove that they were so mentally unstable at the time of the crime that they did not know what they were doing or did not know it was wrong. In the late 19th century some courts adopted the *irresistible impulse test,* under which people who committed crimes in a fit of passion were considered insane. The *Durham test,* which stated that a person was not criminally responsible for an act that was a product of mental disease or defect, was used for a time, but the criteria proved to be too broad. The American Law Institute's solution was to specify that criminal behavior could not be cited as evidence of a mental defect. More recently the federal courts and about half of the state courts have returned to the test of whether the defendant "appreciated the wrongfulness" of the criminal act. Several states now permit a verdict of "guilty but mentally ill." Persons who receive this verdict are sentenced to prison and receive psychological treatment. Some states allow a verdict of "guilty with diminished responsibility." In some states persons repeatedly found guilty of certain sex crimes are categorized as "mentally disordered sex offenders" and are committed to a mental health facility. A growing number of states are abandoning this designation, as it calls for a difficult judgment and is subject to discrimination in its application.

Persons who show signs of mental disturbance and are thought to be dangerous to themselves or others may be forced to undergo treatment under a process of *civil commitment*. The Supreme Court has ruled that there must be "clear and convincing proof" of mental illness before a person can be committed involuntarily. If two physicians certify that a person is dangerous to self or others, the person can be committed immediately. Most mentally disturbed persons are not violent, and future violence is very difficult to predict. Critics charge that involuntary commitment has little therapeutic value and is too easily abused.

Most prominent among *patients' rights* are the right to treatment and the right to refuse treatment. The courts have ruled that states must provide treatment to persons committed involuntarily. Conversely, patients cannot be forced to undergo psychosurgery, and in some states they can refuse ECT and psychotropic medications. Patients also have the right to payment for work they perform, to live in "adult homes" upon release, and to be treated in the least restrictive facility their condition warrants. Critics charge that the exercise of these rights can deprive patients of their chances for recovery and can disrupt effective token economy programs. Advocates of patients' rights reply that because clinicians have so frequently ordered excessive and harmful treatments and have such a poor record of predicting both patients' dangerousness and the effects of their treatments, impartial evaluators must play significant roles in these decisions.

Therapists are increasingly subject to malpractice suits for sexual activity with patients, failure to obtain informed consent for treatment, negligence in administering drugs, improper termination of treatment, and wrongful commitment. At the same time, lawyers are increasingly seeking their help in the selection of jurors.

The line between psychiatrists and psychologists is blurring. Psychologists can now receive Medicare payments and admit patients to the hospitals of some states, and are lobbying for the authority to prescribe drugs.

Each profession within the mental health field has a code of ethics. Psychologists may now offer advice to the public at large provided they do so responsibly; they may not fabricate, distort, misrepresent, or bias their research findings or suppress disconfirming data; they may not have sexual contact with a patient; and they must keep confidential all information they obtain from patients. In some states, however, therapists must disclose a patient's threat to harm an identifiable person.

Mental health professionals also interact with business and economic institutions. They run *employee assistance programs* designed to prevent psychological problems from interfering with work performance, and *stress-reduction* and *problem-solving seminars* designed to teach coping strategies and problem-solving and stress-reduction techniques to employees at all levels.

Private insurance companies, increasingly called upon to pay for mental health services, have instituted a *peer review system* in an effort to cut costs. Many therapists and clients claim that the required reports breach confidentiality and that therapy is shortened to patients' detriment.

KEY TERMS

criminal commitment

M'Naghten rule

irresistible impulse test

Durham test

civil commitment

patients' rights

employee assistance programs

problem-solving seminars

stress reduction seminars

peer review system

SAMPLE MULTIPLE-CHOICE QUESTIONS

1. Persons who are judged to be mentally unstable are regarded by the courts as:
   a. not responsible for their actions
   b. incapable of defending themselves in court
   c. both a and b
   d. neither a nor b

2. Until recent years, most courts chose between which two criteria in determining the sanity of criminal defendants?
   a. M'Naghten and irresistible impulse
   b. Durham and M'Naghten
   c. irresistible impulse and Robinson
   d. Durham and Robinson

3. The Durham test held that individuals are not criminally responsible if their unlawful act was the product of
   a. a psychosis
   b. an irresistible impulse
   c. mental disease or mental defect
   d. a DSM-I diagnosis

4. What diagnosis is received by the majority of defendants
    who are acquitted of a crime by reason of insanity?
    a. antisocial personality disorder
    b. post-traumatic stress disorder
    c. bipolar disorder
    d. schizophrenia

5. A verdict of guilty but mentally ill allows a court:
    a. to ensure treatment if necessary
    b. to impose a prison term
    c. both a and b
    d. neither a nor b

6. The legal system permits involuntary commitment of
    persons who:
    a. are in need of treatment
    b. are dangerous to themselves or others
    c. both a and b
    d. neither a nor b

7. Two-physician certificates apply to which of the
    following situations?
    a. incompetence to stand trial
    b. judgment of a psychosis
    c. judgment of diminished capacity
    d. emergency commitment

8. Research on the prediction of violent behavior has
    shown that the predictions of:
    a. psychiatrists were most accurate
    b. psychologists were most accurate
    c. several clinicians combined were most accurate
    d. none of the above

9. In the case of Wyatt v. Stickney, a federal court ruled
    that when a person had been committed involuntarily,
    the state was obligated to:
    a. provide legal counsel
    b. provide adequate treatment
    c. provide reasonable contact with relatives
    d. all of the above

10. Most courts have upheld the right to refuse:
    a. token economy programs
    b. biological treatments
    c. group psychotherapy
    d. self-government programs

SAMPLE
SHORT-ANSWER
QUESTIONS

1. When individuals accused of a crime are judged to be mentally unstable, they may be sent to a mental institution for treatment under a process of_____.

2. People who are subjected to criminal commitment are judged to be mentally unstable either at the time of _____ or at the time of _____.

3. The rule that defendants were insane at the time of a criminal act if they did not know that the act was wrong is called the _____.

4. Some courts became dissatisfied with the M'Naghten rule and adopted instead the _____.

5. The problem with the Durham test was that the criteria proved to be too _____.

6. The American Law Institute formulated a plan that combined elements of which three tests of insanity?

   _____
   _____
   _____

7. After the Hinckley verdict, there was a movement to return to the _____ standard.

8. Although a few states have abolished the insanity plea (not guilty by reason of insanity), several other states now permit a verdict of _____.

9. A verdict of "guilty with diminished responsibility" has been generally (accepted? not accepted?).

   _____

10. The case of *Dusky* v. *United States* dealt with the issue of incompetence to _____.

11. In *Jackson* v. *Indiana* the Supreme Court ruled that a chronically disordered person could not be committed under criminal status _____.

12. Individuals are forced to undergo treatment through the process of _____.

13. The state's authority to commit individuals rests on two principles:

   _____

   _____

14. The rights of patients that have received the most attention in recent years are

   _____ and

   _____.

15. In the case of _____ the Supreme Court ruled that the state cannot constitutionally confine a nondangerous person who is capable of surviving alone or with family or friends.

16. State rulings have consistently granted patients the right to refuse which biological treatment?

   _____

17. Currently states differ with respect to recognizing a right to refuse _____.

18. The court ruling that protects patients from being taken advantage of by requiring payment of the minimum wage for work performed might well impair the effectiveness of _____ _____ programs.

19. The Tarasoff case concerned client-therapist

   _____.

20. Private insurance companies, in their efforts to monitor what they are paying for, have instituted a

   _____.

EXPLANATIONS OF DIFFICULT MATERIAL

The courts are concerned about a defendant's competence to stand trial because the Constitution guarantees that all persons who are accused of a crime will be given an opportunity to defend themselves in court. Obviously, people who are mentally incompetent may not be able to do so. Yet, there are several problems with the incompetence defense. One problem is that defendants judged to be incompetent may spend a longer time in a mental health facility than they would have spent in prison if they had been tried and convicted of the crime. Society was responsive to this problem, and the Supreme Court ruled that after a reasonable length of time the defendant must either be tried, set free, or civilly committed. Another problem is that a person may fake incompetence as a way of avoiding or delaying court action. Yet such faking is thought to occur very infrequently, and most instances of it are detected. Thus it seems that, on balance, the constitutional protection against requiring people to stand trial if they are incompetent to participate in their defense is an important one to maintain, despite occasional problems.

ADDITIONAL READINGS

Appelbaum, P. S. (1988). The right to refuse treatment with antipsychotic medications: Retrospect and prospect. *American Journal of Psychiatry, 145,* 413–419.

Klassen, D., & O'Connor, W. A. (1988). Predicting violence in schizophrenic and non-schizophrenic patients: A prospective study. *Journal of Community Psychology, 16,* 217–227.

Melton, G. B. (Ed.) (1987). *Reforming the law: Impact of child development research.* New York: Guilford.

Melton, G. B., Weithorn, L. A., & Slobogin, C. (1985). *Community mental health centers.* Lincoln: University of Nebraska Press.

Morris, A., & Tomroy, M. (Eds.) (1983). *Crime and justice: An annual review of research.* Chicago: University of Chicago Press.

Mulvey, E. P., Geller, J. L., & Roth, L. H. (1987). The promise and peril of involuntary outpatient commitment. *American Psychologist, 42,* 571–584.

Phillips, M. R., & Wolf, A. S. (1988). Psychiatry and the criminal justice system: Testing and myths. *American Journal of Psychiatry, 145,* 605–610.

Scheflin, A. W., & Shapiro, A. M. (1989). *Trance on trial.* New York: Guilford.

Scheirer, C. J., & Hammond, B. L. (Eds.) (1983). *Psychology and the law.* Washington, D.C.: American Psychological Association.

Steadman, H. J. (1981). The statistical prediction of violent behavior: Measuring the costs of a public protectionist versus a civil libertarian model. *Law and Human Behavior, 5,* 263–274.

ANSWER KEY

Multiple-Choice Questions:

1c, 2a, 3c, 4d, 5c, 6c, 7d, 8d, 9b, 10b.

Short-Answer Questions:

1. criminal commitment
2. the crime; the trial
3. M'Naghten rule
4. irresistible impulse test
5. broad
6. M'Naghten, irresistible impulse, Durham
7. M'Naghten (or wrongfulness)
8. guilty but mentally ill
9. not accepted
10. stand trial
11. indefinitely
12. civil commitment
13. *parens patriae*, police power
14. the right to treatment, the right to refuse treatment
15. *O'Connor v. Donaldson*
16. psychosurgery
17. ECT (electroconvulsive therapy)
18. token economy
19. confidentiality
20. peer review system